The Monsters Family
It's Not "Just Business"

By Andrew Funk
with Deborah Kevin

ISBN 9781656794864

This book is dedicated to my brother, Alan.

You taught me to laugh, to fight for what's right, and to dream big.
Without you, I wouldn't be who I am today.

Table of Contents

Introduction

When I look back on my journey to become an entrepreneur, it seems now like an obvious outcome. But, back when I was in high school, and my future mother-in-law suggested that I become a business owner, I scoffed. *No way*, I thought. *I see how hard you're working all the time. I don't want that kinda life.*

Boy, was I ever wrong (well, maybe not about the hard work part)! That's why they say we have 20/20 vision in hindsight.

My journey from roller rink snack bar counter critter to CEO of a world-renowned hip hop dance convention has been fraught with challenges, all of which grew and continue to grow me. This is the story of me finding my way to lead a movement, a tale that has never before been told as I'm not a guy who likes the spotlight but prefers to highlight the achievements of others.

So why now? I'm about to open my proverbial kimono for you to see what's worked, what flopped, and what I've learned about family and business because, for me, Monsters of HipHop is not "just business."

Peace,

Andy

1: Generational Funk

"Cherish these nights,
cherish these people.
Life is a movie,
but there'll never be a sequel."
Nicki Minaj

I grew up, the second of two sons, in historic Gettysburg, located in south-central Pennsylvania. My hometown was as big on small-town charm as it was in Civil War reenactments. Our extended family was close-knit, which was and continues to be a blessing.

My parents, Joyce and Gene, have been the best parents a kid could ever hope for–and I was quite a handful as a child. The doctors declared that I was hyperactive and prescribed medications to calm my outbursts. Turns out, there was more to it than that because I would often feel weak and faint. Ultimately, I underwent a lengthy series of glucose tests that uncovered the real source of my issues: I was hypoglycemic. From that point on, I kept a snack with me at all times, and any time I started to feel like passing out, I ate a granola bar, an orange, or drank juice to stabilize my blood sugar.

In second grade, I tested into a gifted and talented program because I was bored in many of my classes (and a bored, hyperactive kid isn't fun to teach!). I stayed in the program through sixth grade, but hated leaving my regular classes–and my friends–to attend special GT classes at a house down the street from my school, so I opted out.

I lived with my parents and older brother Alan in a small, white three-bedroom rancher. The smallest bedroom in our house was mine, and it was filled with books, even though, as a kid, I didn't enjoy reading. My beloved boombox sat on a bedside table, as music played a huge role in my childhood. I loved rock and hip hop, which I listened to on 98.5 WYCR. The few Beastie Boys and Van Halen cassette tapes I owned I played so often that the sound became warped.

The problem with relying on my boom box was that it wasn't something I could transport easily on the school bus. So I did what any self-respecting kid in those days did: I made tape recordings of my favorite songs from the radio, perfecting the fine art of pausing the recording just as the D.J. started to talk, then I played those tapes on my Sony Walkman on the school bus. Nirvana!

Childhood home in Gettysburg, PA.

I didn't have a chance to listen to much more than what I was allowed to get on the radio, but I made up for it later in life, catching up mostly with a lot of hip hop from the '80s and early '90s and, of course, plenty of hair band rock.

I loved music so much that I nearly didn't graduate from eighth grade. The station I listened to, 98YCR, had an afternoon segment where callers could "flush" someone or something. As a joke, I called the station to "flush" my school. Of course, I used my boombox to record the call, which I proceeded to talk about and share with my friends the next day at school.

It was all meant in good fun, except that I went to a Catholic School named Sacred Heart, and when my teacher caught wind of the conversation, she immediately referred me to the Principal's office. Because my intentions were purely fun, and I meant no harm, I willingly played my tape for the Principal, who was a nun.

Sister said, "Andrew, you're a disgrace!" Then threatened legal action to prevent me from graduating in a few weeks.

"I'm so sorry," I said, realizing that I'd made a poor choice (whether to 'flush' my school or brag about it, I'm still not sure—it was pretty funny). "I'm sorry!"

After some heated meetings where my parents came to my defense, the incident somehow blew over, and I was able to graduate as planned. Whew!

What I remember most about our home was that it always smelled like whatever amazing food my mom was cooking. Even Oodles of Noodles smelled extra delicious because she would cut fresh chives from her garden to spruce it up.

Between my parents and grandmothers, *we ate!* Roast beef dinners with homemade mashed potatoes, spaghetti casserole, and even some odd concoctions that I was forced to try made for many happy bellies.

Some of my favorite childhood memories come from time spent with my family on Thanksgiving and Easter. I sorely miss those days! Grandma Kerrigan prepared a literal feast. Perfectly roasted turkey, mashed potatoes, sweet potatoes, corn, corn casserole, green beans, cranberry everything, and PIES. She served pumpkin pie, apple pie (with and without raisins), peach pie, rhubarb pie (yuck!), cherry, blueberry, coconut, and egg custard pies. The entire family on my Mom's side would gather at my grandma's house, eat themselves to bursting, and then pass out from food comas.

Summertime picnics were a staple at our house when I was grow-ing up. Mom made fresh-brewed mint tea from the leaves she picked from our backyard. There were deviled eggs with a sprinkle of paprika on top, hot dogs and burgers on the grill (occasionally some juicy BBQ chicken), and a variety of traditional family casseroles and some salads that I'd have to eat.

"Just try it," Mom said.

We'd play Wiffle ball, volleyball, badminton, and horseshoes. After everyone left and we cleaned up, my brother Alan and I would play baseball until it was dangerously dark, and Mom or Dad would call us in. Summers were generally uneventful.

There was one afternoon when my brother and I were fooling around with a five iron in the backyard. We were not golfers; I didn't actually step on a real golf course until my Junior year in high school, which was slightly embarrassing because no one told me that you couldn't "tee" it up in the fairway or from the rough, which is where I spent most of my time.

I don't recall most of the details of this particular afternoon, and those that I do apparently did not occur exactly as they are indelibly marked in my brain. Alan and I were taking turns chipping a golf ball. Our yard wasn't very big, so anything greater than chipping would have undoubtedly ended up having a ball go through a neighbor's window.

On one particular back swing, I hit something that felt oddly differ-ent. Here's where my recollection gets a little imaginative. My memory tells me it went like this (cue a calming David Feherty voice), "Young Andrew lines up for what should be an easy chip shot to the green. A slow, deep breath and gentle half practice swing..."

At this point, Bob Menery's outrageous commentary takes over. "Holy %#ck! Andrew just rammed that five-iron straight between his brother's eyes. The whole f@c#*% blade is sticking out of Alan's forehead! There's blood gushing everywhere. Oh, my gosh! Alan pulled the club right out, and now he's chasing his little brother around the fairway."

Here's what really happened: My five-iron did connect with Alan's head, giving him a nice divot. The sight of blood completely traumatized me, and the thought that Alan might bleed to death because of me had me running around the yard, screaming like a little baby for my parents. My brother remained fairly calm and survived, with only a few stitches.

Outside of our brotherly backyard shenanigans, I was very active growing up. I started playing soccer around the age of four and also took up drumming around the same time.

My mom was an art teacher early on, so I enjoyed a variety of art programs at local colleges.

Of course, there was also a lot of roller skating between the late '70s and early '80s at my grandparent's roller skating rink. Time at the Rink definitely solidified my love for music. Prince, Lionel Ritchie, Cyndi Lauper, Journey, and Earth, Wind & Fire replayed in my head all week until I'd get back to the rink each weekend. I can't leave out Toni Basil's 1981 hit "Mickey." Little did I know back then that I would have an opportunity to meet and work with Toni many years later.

Looking back, I'd say my first decade of life was pretty cool.

But that's where my childhood ends.

2: Alan

"You've got to realize the world's a test,
You can only do your best and let Him do the rest.
You've got your life, you've got your health,
So quit procrastinating and push it yourself."
Cee-Lo Green

Most of the memories I have of my older brother Alan are from after he got sick. I was eleven when we learned that he had leukemia. I hate it, but most of what I recall is of hospitals, baldness, vomiting, doctors, IV bags, and driving back and forth to Hershey Medical Center. In spite of all he endured, Alan kept his witty and mischievous side present and accounted for.

Scattered in between are memories of our picnics, playing just about anything we could outside, and building snow forts in the winter.

Once, Alan and I, along with four or five other neighborhood kids, used red plastic brick molds to build a two-room snow fort. It took us all day. I recall hunkering down inside and marveling that I actually felt warm, even though I'm certain it must have been freezing!

We also had some epic snowball fights, which nearly always ended up with me getting hit in the face and running inside, crying about how Alan and his friends had been mean to me.

Like many older brothers, Alan was known for scaring me. One bright, sunny afternoon, I played in my room, and Alan was in his.

"Andy," Alan whispered just loud enough for me to hear him.

"Come see me."

I dropped what I was doing and walked into his room. I found him completely covered, head-to-toe, with a sheet.

Slowly, very slowly, he sat up, all the while chanting, "I am the witch with the silver dollar eyyyyyeeessss." When the sheet fell off his face, two silver dollars covered his eyes.

I screamed in terror, which, when I think back on it, makes me laugh a little nostalgically. At the time, I felt pure terror.

You might think that when Alan got sick, his pranks stopped, but you'd be wrong. One time when he had an extremely low blood count, he devised a scheme to freak our mom out.

"Andy," he said. "Go get me the ketchup from the 'frig."

I dutifully retrieved the Heinz bottle and handed it over to him. He proceeded to douse his white tee-shirt with the red sauce, rubbing some across his neck.

"Now," Alan said, "Go run and tell mom that I'm bleeding. And act like it's an emergency!"

I once again followed his orders, rushing up to my mom, yelling, "Come quick! Alan's bleeding all over the place!"

Mom took one look at Alan and burst into tears, calling for our Dad to come quick. She grabbed a towel to stop the bleeding. She quickly realized she'd been horribly pranked.

I'm sure the whole incident lasted only a few minutes, but we suffered for a lot longer after that. I don't recall what the punishment was, but I know we both felt terrible afterward.

My parents were simply amazing throughout my brother's illness, sheltering me from the details of what was going on. It's likely a blessing that I only retained a superficial recollection of the events.

Alan had been sick for a couple of weeks, a lingering cold or flu. He just couldn't kick it. Our family doctor ordered a blood test to see what was going on.

One afternoon we were at Grandma Kerrigan's when either my

Mom or Grandma received a call that prompted a hurried trip to Hershey Medical Center. Alan's most recent blood work was troubling.

That was the first time that I spent with my Grandma or Pap without my parents for something other than a fun sleepover. I had a vague awareness that "Alan was very sick."

I felt scared, confused, and my stomach ached. I wondered what the heck was going on and where Alan was. I didn't ask many questions, and no one said much about it. I just felt a seriousness about the situation.

A day or two after that call came in, my Dad picked me up and took me to visit Alan in Hershey. I vaguely remember walking into the front door of the huge research hospital, still unsure of what I was walking into. I'm sure my dad and I talked on the 55-minute car ride to the hospital, but about what I couldn't tell you. I'm pretty sure I had several dozen rides like that over the next couple of years as Alan rode back and forth each day for chemo.

I'm not exactly sure who explained to me that Alan had been diagnosed with Acute Lymphocytic Leukemia (ALL)–it may have been a social worker. I was told Alan would need to stay in the hospital for several weeks to receive chemotherapy. The pamphlet I was given didn't answer my deepest questions, ones I was terrified to voice. I pretended not to think too much about it, but the body knows better!

As Alan received his treatment, I woke several times for school to discover I felt sick, too. My stomach hurt, my head ached, and I felt nauseated. Calling out sick from school meant I could trek with my mom and brother to Hershey. While he received his treatments, I did school work. I'm pretty sure I wasn't really sick–funny how I always felt better once we got home–but worry and stress show up in funny ways sometimes (a lesson I keep revisiting). Seeing my big brother lose his hair, swell from Prednisone, and vomit most days took a toll on all of us for sure. By the time I was fourteen, I had a pre-ulcerative stomach irritation that required medication.

The time after Alan was diagnosed, probably for more than a year or two, remains a blur.

I spent countless hours with both sets of my grandparents, and they created a sense of normalcy during a surreal time when my brother Alan was hospitalized. How lucky was I to have them in my life well into adulthood and have them attend both my college graduation and wedding? They lived to meet two out of my three sons.

During the most intense times of Alan's treatment, my Mom would stay with him in the hospital while my Dad still had to work. I rotated weeks at my grandparents, staying one week at Grandma and PapPap Kerrigan's house in Gettysburg and the next at Grandma and PapPaw Funk's in Irishtown. (I always thought it was ironic that the German Funks lived in Irishtown, and the Irish Kerrigans lived in Gettysburg.)

My grandfather, Charles Kerrigan, a decorated World War II veteran and champion horseshoe player, married my grandmother, Grace, in 1948. They were happily married for sixty years and died in 2009 within six months of each other.

While I called my grandfather Pap, others knew him best as "Junie" or "Kerrigan, the Painter," because of his successful painting business, which he ran for over forty years. He and my grandmother also owned the popular Gettysburg Roller Rink, which they operated for fifteen years.

Grandma & PapPap Kerrigan at the Gettysburg Roller Rink

Kerrigan The Painter

Man, that rink was a fun place to be their grandson. I liked to skate fast, and Louie, the figure skater who trained and taught there, was not happy about it. I was a skinny, little skate rat who would skate forward and backward, swerving in between people.

Louie would complain to the skate guard, who would blow his whistle and tell me to slow down.

I'd snap back, "You can't tell me what to do, my grandparents own this place."

Then, Grandma or Pap would call me into the office to help spray sanitizer into the skates when they were returned. My head would spin from the rotating smells of stinky feet and odorizer.

As quickly as I could, I'd make my way to the snack bar for frozen shoestring French fries and a bag of Swedish Fish. Sounds crazy, I know, but I loved the taste of frozen fries straight out of the paper bag. Of course, the fried ones were tasty, too.

Friday night sock hops with the live DJ were the best, although that's really when I had to avoid the floor for the slow skates because girls were still gross at that point in my life. Regular Saturday morning or afternoon skates didn't present the same kind of problem.

When I was a kid, Pap would often take me to Ernie's Texas Lunch, where we'd order Coke and a couple of *hot dogs with everything, lite onions.* So many people greeted my grandfather on the streets that, for many years, I thought he must be the town's mayor! Turns out, he was "only" the fire chief.

Time spent at Grandma and Pap Kerrigan's was a lot different from Grandma and PapPaw Funk's, and I think it had a lot to do with them running the family businesses out of the house. The phone rang a lot. People would often just stop by with a payment, interrupting my Scooby-Doo cartoon watching. Or I'd run errands to Woolworth's with one of them for supplies. Along with their businesses and taking care of me, my grandmother also babysat my cousins, Julie and Justin. Life there could be described as organized chaos, which I would later come to know very well in my own life.

When I stayed at Grandma and PapPaw Funk's, there was a comfortable and predictable routine, including sitting in the same chairs at mealtimes.

Grandma Funk was famous for her Swiss steak and broken glass for dessert, which was a combination of visual art and deliciousness made with crushed graham crackers and cubes of different colored jello, all smothered in whipped cream. It was amazing! (Maybe my next book ought to be all our family recipes. Yes?)

PapPaw Funk, also a Veteran and Purple Heart recipient, worked full-time as an electrician while Grandma worked at the Hanover Shoe Factory. After my school day ended, I'd go to their house, where there was always a snack and drink while I'd do my homework and rocked out to music blaring on my Walkman. By then, I had added Run DMC and Metallica to my tape collection!

When my homework was finished, I'd watch cartoons, help Grandma with laundry, or work with Pap on woodworking projects. After dinner, we'd play cards before turning on Pap's and my favorite cartoons: Mighty Mouse and Looney Tunes. The night ended with me listening to Grandma and Pap singing along to Hee Haw and saying the rosary before going to bed.

While time spent with both sets of my grandparents were different experiences, I cherish them equally. I learned many of the most important life lessons from them, like unconditional love, the value of hard work and sacrifice, and one I cherish the most, appreciate whatever you have, big or small.

I also occasionally spent the night at my Aunt Sus's home. Susie, as many of her friends called her, was one of my favorite people in the world, and she had the biggest heart of anyone I've ever met. Never married, she spoiled all of her nieces and nephews, especially at Christmas (you should have seen the towering piles of gifts!).

Aunt Sus was one of those people in town whom everyone knew and loved! She worked the snack bar at the roller skating rink and would put me to work every time a slow song came on, thus saving me from having to couple skate with a girl.

Friday nights after the rink closed, we would all go back to my grandparents' house, and order from Tommy's a regular cheese, pepperoni, hamburger, and onion pizza. We'd gulp down Pepsi, which was the fuel for some EPIC belch battles. We took turns to see who could produce the loudest, longest, and most creative burps. Aunt Sus would destroy all of us—such were her many talents!

We also played on the shag rug a game we called "tackle-backle," our fancy name for wrestling. We'd wrestle until either someone was about to puke, they hit their head on the coffee table, or we knocked over a collectible of Grandma's salt and pepper shaker collection. Whoops!

Anyways, those times with my grandparents provided a much-needed diversion from the reality of what my brother was going through and kept me as focused as possible on just moving onward.

When school was out, Grandma and Pap and I would take the long drive from Gettysburg to Hershey in his cream-colored Oldsmobile to visit Alan. I hated that drive but loved the smell of that car, the back seats were so plush and comfy, it felt a little like a hug.

Visits to the Hershey Medical Center seemed to last hours. I spent hours playing Asteroids and Galaga on the arcade machine in the playroom on the fifth floor until the day turned into night. The social work staff were exceptional and looked after me, playing games and doing crafts with me to pass the time.

I knew Alan was sick, but it always just seemed like a matter of time until he'd be home and life would return to normal. As kids, we think in simple and sometimes magical terms. To think anything other than Alan would get well never occurred to me. My parents made sure to stay positive, too.

On weekends, I stayed with my dad at the Ronald McDonald House across the street from the medical center, and it truly became a home-away-from-home for a few years. My dad and I cheered on our beloved Penn State Nittany Lions as they won National Championship in 1986. We screamed and shouted at the television in the living room at the Ronald McDonald House, and for a few times, the reason we were there and not at home disappeared.

The Ronald McDonald House provided normalcy for us, and, in some ways, those times even felt like a vacation in some strange way. I thank God every day for having stayed there.

A generous manager of the Ronald McDonald House, Ben, surprised me on more than one occasion with tickets to see events at the nearby Hershey Arena. Once when my dad and I returned from visiting Alan, we found an envelope waiting for us. Inside were WWF tickets and a letter directing us to a specific arena door where we could meet some of the wrestlers. Bob Orton took on Mr. Wonderful that night in a cast match. Disappointingly, Hulk Hogan was supposed to meet us, but he ended up not feeling well.

Alan went in and out of remission a few times, but in 1987 when leukemia had returned stronger and quicker than before, things changed. At that point, the doctors presented our family with one last option: a bone marrow transplant. At the time, bone marrow transplants were still somewhat experimental, and the most successful transplants were happening in Seattle, Washington, and Iowa City, Iowa. My parents decided on Iowa because of its closer proximity to home.

But first, Alan needed a donor.

My parents and I were tested first to see if any of us were good matches for him. At the same time, there was another family who had a child in need of bone marrow. They had eleven people tested, and none of them was a close enough match. The stakes felt high.

The results came back, and only one of us was a match for Alan: me. *Finally!* I felt like I could do something meaningful to help him, even though I had no concept of what it meant to donate bone marrow.

The doctor explained to my parents, Alan, and me what would happen. Then he looked at me and said, "The transplant might not work. If it doesn't, it's not your fault."

As I'm writing this thirty-two years later, I'm just now realizing what they were trying to tell me, although these words were never spoken: Alan might still die.

Before the transplant, Alan had to endure a few days of intense chemo and radiation therapy, which ravaged his body to prepare it to receive the new marrow. The process was intended to reboot his system. The thinking back then was that the patient had to be completely in remission from the reboot before receiving the transplanted marrow.

We arrived at the hospital in Iowa City one morning, anticipating the bone marrow transplant to take place. One last blood test showed that Alan had "blasts" or cancer cells yet again.

Dr. Trigg, a pioneer in the bone marrow transplant field, had gotten to know my brother and our family quite well in the days leading up to the transplant. He spoke to us about what would happen next. "With cancer cells still showing up, it's an option to go home without the transplant to enjoy the time you have left."

I heard my mom sniffle and felt a little better, knowing that I wasn't the only one crying. Alan didn't cry, though.

Dr. Trigg said, "Or because you have such a positive attitude, you could decide to go for it." He paused and looked Alan straight in his eyes. "Even with the transplant, your long term survival rate is between zero and ten percent."

Alan didn't flinch. "It's the same boat, just a little smaller, that's all."

And with that, the *meeting was adjourned*, and we pulled ourselves together to prepare for the transplant.

For the first time as a patient, I spent the night before the transplant in the hospital. I felt nervous and also oddly super excited. The next morning, I saw Alan, kissed Mom and Dad, and took a ride to the operating room. I had agreed to just have an epidural, numbing me from my waist down. I thought it would be cool to be awake during the procedure, and the P.A.'s (Physician's Assistants) had games planned to keep me occupied throughout.

As I was wheeled into the room, my eyes landed on trays of scalpels, huge syringes with needles several inches long, and other horrifying hardware laying open on the blue paper-covered tray.

I felt queasy. "Nevermind! Put me out."

As they placed the mask on my face to let me drift off to sleep, my last vision was the P.A. walking in the room, saying, "Nooo." I guess he was looking forward to game time.

When I came out of recovery, the nurse rolled me into Alan's room, where my still-warm marrow was already flowing into his body.

Hopefully, already working to cure him, I thought. At that moment, I felt like a superhero. Shortly after, however, I felt the pain. Bone marrow transplants are no longer what they used to be. Today, it's a same-day surgery, but then they cut about twenty or so small incisions all across my hips and lower back to harvest the marrow. I swear every year around that time, I feel a tinge of backache to remind me of Alan and that time in our lives. It was a fresh start. It was the beginning of Alan's new life.

After the bone marrow transplant, our family lived in an apartment in Coralville, Iowa, for about three months, Alan continued battling cancer, and I went about being a 12-year-old kid, even being kind-of homeschooled. I have no idea what my grades were or what we studied; it seemed most people realized that the life lessons I was experiencing were sufficient.

One of Alan's doctors coached a competitive soccer team and invited me to join. For one season, I played goalie, winning a championship in the capital city along the way.

One thing I know for sure is that the Funk family transformed that Iowa City hospital floor during our time there. To crowd out time for misery or doubt to creep in, Alan and I instigated water gun and water balloon battles, ambushing Dr. Trigg and the staff.

No matter how sick he was, Alan kept up his prankster status. He acquired a pen that had bright blue disappearing ink and squirted the ink on Dr. Trigg's pressed white shirt and long lab coat. The inky stain appeared on his shirt and coat, spreading out to create a Rorschach blot.

Dr. Trigg's face turned red. "What the–!"

Just as quickly as the ink appeared, it began to fade. Dr. Trigg realized Alan had pranked him. They laughed together.

Then there was the time that Alan put a rubber snake in the toilet and closed the lid. A nurse went into the bathroom to collect what she thought was Alan's stool sample. Her screams caused us to double over. Times like that created some of the best medicine...laughter!

Despite the good-natured torture the staff endured at our hands, they loved us. Just like Ben at the Ronald McDonald House had, the hospital workers noticed my interest in wrestling. They somehow procured two tickets so my Dad and I could see Wrestlemania 3 at the Silverdome in Detroit–only the best one *ever*, with Hulk Hogan body-slamming the great Andre the Giant.

I befriended a boy named Patrick, who had also undergone a transplant. He had a great attitude and was the only person close to my age to hang out with during the countless hours we spent at the hospital. The Child Life staff helped facilitate bake sales on the floor with cookies Patrick and I made and an occasional lemonade stand where we hustled nearly everyone. Patrick helped me get through those times as much as I helped him, so it was particularly difficult when my friend ultimately passed away.

Before the transplant, Alan wanted to know how long he would be in the hospital and what to expect, then he set a goal. He broke the record for fewest days in-patient post-transplant at forty-one days, drawing a line through each day on a big calendar in his room until they released him to our apartment.

Three months later, we started our trek home to Pennsylvania in a donated RV. As we rolled into town and arrived home, a crowd of family and friends, as well as news crews, greeted us. It was the best welcome home from Iowa!

Alan went on to graduate high school after missing over half of his high school years in and out of hospitals. He fell in love with Michele Berube, who was a year or so behind him in high school. He moved away to Penn State Altoona, where he talked about studying psychology. He lived life to the fullest, making the best of each new day, partying, and going to Penn State football games in State College.

We missed him terribly, and my parents worried about him constantly. I looked forward to the times when we got the chance to go visit him at school. One time, I stayed in the dorm with him overnight, and that's about all that I'll say about that—because what happened at the dorm, stays at the dorm!

One of the best times Alan had while at Penn State was when he took the stage during THON, which is the largest student-run philanthropy in the world. For forty-six hours straight, Penn State dancers stand and dance to raise funds for the Four Diamonds Fund, an organization that served my family while Alan was sick (https://thon.org/).

THON occurred in February, not too long after Alan's bone marrow transplant. He still wore a wig, which he pulled off while on stage, tossing it into the crowd. He received uproarious applause. To them, at that moment, Alan was a rock star. To say he inspired people during his life is an understatement. I know for a fact that on that day, he moved thousands.

Little did I know that this period in my life was preparing me for what was about to happen next. It was the foundation I would need to draw strength and courage from later on. It ingrained the importance of community and family, positivity.

You know the old saying, "When life gives you lemons?" Well, Alan taught us how to make the lemonade!

Alan & Andy Post-Transplant, 1987

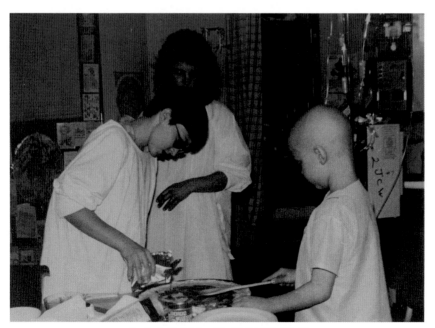

Andy & Patrick with Child Life Staff

Iowa State Soccer Champs, Iowa City

THE TIMES, WEDNESDAY, JUNE 17, 1987

HOME AGAIN — Alan Funk and his family and the principal of his high school stand under a banner at the family home in Bonneauville. Alan had a bone-marrow transplant in March from his brother Andy as part of his battle with leukemia. Alan spent 80 days in the University of Iowa Hospital in Iowa City taking intense chemical and radiation thereapy before he received bone-marrow from his brother's body. He will spend the next several months in semi-conclusion while his immune system recuperates. Pictured (from left) are Joyce Kerrigan Funk, Alan, Andy, Father Michael Grab, principal of Delone Catholic High School, and Gene Funk.

Welcome Home from Iowa

3: Things My Brother Taught Me

"I'm tryna keep my faith
But I'm looking for more
Somewhere I can feel safe
And end my holy war
I'm tryna keep my faith."
Kanye West

Life clicked along normally for almost three years after the transplant. Then, in the fall of his sophomore year, Alan developed a cold. The cold progressed into pneumonia, which led to his lung collapsing several times. Each time, he was rushed to the hospital to have his lung repaired. I say repaired like his lung was a flat tire, and in some ways, it kind of was. The doctors literally stuck a tube into Alan's lung, blew it up, patched it, and sent him on his way.

By the winter of 1990, it became evident that Alan was suffering from the long-term side effects from the mega doses of radiation that he had received before the transplant. With his lungs so weakened, the attempts to fix them were not working.

It was decided Alan would head back to Iowa, where he could receive treatment by Dr. Trigg and the hospital staff there. Mom made the trip with Alan via medical airlift, with Dad and me following two weeks later.

On the flight to Iowa, Mom saw out her window a field of shrubs in the shape of a cross. Even today, that memory stands out to her about that "very strange trip."

Soon after Dad and I arrived in Iowa, Alan underwent a procedure to install a port to more easily administer medication. I didn't know it at the time, but Alan was in bad shape. I thought this is just another bump in the road of his recovery, and he would bounce back.

My mom awaited just outside the operating room while Alan was inside getting the port. My dad and I had stepped out, leaving her alone.

Suddenly, a blue light above the operating room door began flashing.

Over the hospital loudspeaker came a voice saying, "Code Blue,"

A flurry of hospital staff rushed into the OR.

"What's happening?" Mom said to the doctors and nurses hurrying by. She tried to get inside to Alan but wasn't permitted in.

As quickly as the panic began, it ended. Everyone who had rushed into the room calmly walked out, telling my Mom that Alan was okay and cracking jokes. During the procedure, his heart had stopped momentarily.

Hours later, in Alan's hospital room, Dr. Trigg was somber, He said, "The next twenty-four hours will be critical."

The room was dark and felt stuffy. Alan had oxygen tubes in his nose and looked frail, exhausted. The sound of machines beat out a rhythm that mirrored Alan's chest rising and falling.

"Dad," I said. "Can we go back to the hotel?" We were booked into The Canterbury Inn, a modest motel near the hospital where we stayed for our shorter visits to Iowa.

My parents exchanged looks before Dad said, "Let's go." He drove me to the motel, got me settled, and returned to the hospital. I ought to have known something was terribly wrong because it was the first time in my life that my parents had ever left me alone.

I collapsed on my bed and fell into a deep sleep, exhausted from the travel and worry about my brother. I awoke to someone pounding on my door. Disoriented, I looked at the clock. It read 1:00 a.m. Rubbing the sleep from my eyes, I stumbled to the door.

Steve Rummelhart, the P.A. who had planned to play games with me during my bone marrow harvesting, stood outside. "Andy, let's get you back to the hospital."

I grabbed my glasses and shoved my shoes on, running behind Steve to his car.

As he pulled onto the road, Steve said, "We don't think Alan is going to make it through the night."

The words landed like bricks on my heart. I couldn't make sense of them. For five years, Alan had faced—and conquered—all kinds of life-threatening situations. Never once had I contemplated that he might die. He was bigger than cancer. Stronger than cancer. He would beat it.

Steve escorted me to the room. The lights were dim, and classical music played softly. Pachebel's Canon in D. The room felt freezing cold. I shivered.

Alan lay on the bed, tubes everywhere—so many more than when his lung collapsed. An oxygen mask covered half his face, and I could see that his breathing was labored. I walked over and gave him a hug.

"You're going to make it, Alan," I said. "Keep fighting."

No one stopped me from making that plea, they allowed me my grief. I wasn't ready to let my big brother go, and they all knew it. Over the next hour, I paced around the room. I paced in the hallway, circling back every few moments to give Alan some encouragement.

His breathing grew raspy. It sounded like he was suffocating (because he was). Each breath announced agonizing pain. I can't even imagine how he held on for so long.

"Please give him something," my parents begged the nurses. "He's suffering!"

I believe Alan was hanging on until Mom, Dad, and I told him it was okay to go. His tolerance for pain and will to protect me was incredible.

We sat for about four hours, though it felt like much longer. Earlier the day before, Alan made the decision on his own to forego life support. He was worn out and tired. Even then, he was looking out for us by making the decision on his own, so we wouldn't have to do it later.

He must have known, even before I left for the Canterbury, that he was probably going to die.

The staff made phone calls and tried to get authorizations, but as I understand it, one of the doctors had such a hard time that he went to another floor to avoid the reality of seeing Alan dying. Alan Funk was larger than life for many who knew him even at that moment.

At one point, Alan began coughing up brown blood, which made it even more difficult for him to catch his breath. The signs all pointed to the end of his fight, and after much pleading, more medications arrived that would help him rest.

Alan couldn't speak any longer, so he scribbled words onto paper my dad held for him. He wrote, "What's in the pump?" He was so smart and intuitive, and he knew that whatever they were about to inject into his pump was going to help ease him through his death.

I leaned in and kissed his cheek. It felt so cold beneath my lips. I whispered, my voice catching on the words, "I love you. It's okay to go. We'll be fine."

Alan looked into my eyes, probably seeking confirmation that my words were true.

I sobbed and nodded my head. I didn't know how we'd survive this, but I knew we would.

Alan raised his hand to pull his oxygen mask away from his mouth just long enough to say, "I love you guys."

Mom, Dad, and I gathered close, hugging him, and each other. Alan continued to stare at us.

A nurse listened to his chest with a stethoscope and took his pulse. Alan's chest continued to rise and fall, but more peacefully. Everything moved in slow motion.

At 5:55 a.m., the nurse reached up and switched off the monitors. Then, she left the room.

Alan was gone.

We sat there in shock. Numbness set in. Tears flowed. I needed some air and asked my parents if I could go for a walk.

I ambled aimlessly through the halls my brother, and I had wandered together, eventually sitting in the lounge area.

An orderly walked into the room, dropping coins into the vending machine. "Are you okay?" he asked.

"My brother just died," I said.

"I'm so sorry," he said. "Let me send someone in to help you."

After he left, I went to the payphone and dialed my girlfriend Becky's number. "He's gone," I said into the receiver. My tears were all gone, and I felt flat, deflated.

"I know," Becky said, her voice thick with tears. We had only been dating about five months at that point, but she was there for me every step of the way, especially then when I needed her the most.

We went back to the Canterbury Inn one last time to sleep for a while. The silence was palpable. The hotel blinds were pulled against the rising sun, creating this weird half-light/half-dark effect in the room. It reflected our feelings perfectly.

On the flight back to BWI, Mom sat in silence with Alan's photograph on her lap. All I could think about was that my brother's body was beneath us in a box deep within the plane's belly.

We were once again greeted at the airport by family and friends. There were hugs and tears and deep silence. So much silence. It felt a little like the world's lights had dimmed. People were so kind, but I felt like I was wrapped in cotton. Nothing much permeated the fuzziness. I dove back into band, schoolwork, soccer, and dating Becky.

My big brother died at nineteen, just one month shy of his twentieth birthday. His fight and zest for life were brilliant to behold. I'm still in awe of his courage. His playfulness and intelligence are two of the many things I miss daily. Who he was and how he shaped my life resulted in my willingness to take risks–certainly calculated business risks– and try things others might question, and serve others at the highest level. In some ways, I feel I owe it to him since he didn't get to live to be an old man. He may not have had enough time, but he certainly made the most of what time he did have.

I think I've always felt an unspoken pressure to do good, make the best of my life, and have some sort of positive impact on my world (insert the tiny voice that says, "since Alan didn't have a chance to"). No one else put that pressure on me–only me. I felt the need to fill my time working on something or planning something. It is somewhat of an affliction, I think because I don't often sleep well at night thinking about what needs to get done next or wondering if I'm doing enough.

While I still struggle with this at times, I have begun to make a conscious effort to slow down and just breathe. I have come to realize now, that I'm doing the best I can with my kids, my work, and my community. I think Alan would be proud–and that's cool with me!

4: Love of My Life

"When I see you smile, I see a ray of light.
Oh, oh, I see it shining right through the rain."
Bad English

I remember vividly the first time I laid eyes on Becky Servant. I was in my percussion instructor's apartment, and Becky's framed school photo sat on a side table. She wore a beret and braces, but it was the sparkle in her blue eyes and dimples that caught my attention. I was in sixth grade and was among a handful of middle schoolers who had been recruited by the high school marching band to fill their ranks. My brother Alan had played the trumpet in the band, too.

Lori Thompson (LT) was my percussion instructor at Delone Catholic, and her long-time girlfriend/partner was Gina Servant, who worked with the band's color guard. Gina and LT had invited the drumline and color guard to their college apartment to celebrate the end of the year. LT and Gina, along with the entire school and band community, had been incredibly supportive of Alan and our family, so the band was like a second home for me.

Shortly after arriving at the party, I came across a picture of Gina's younger sister Becky. I had seen her around with Gina and Lori, but her picture drew me in like a moth to a flame. I kept walking by and staring at it, hoping to appear casual. I don't remember if I asked about the girl in the photo or if Gina and LT noticed my interest. Either way, it was clear I was smitten. And I held that image in my mind's eye until four years later when we finally exchanged more than a few awkward words.

Becky walked into the band room, a long, narrow room with several riser levels. The percussion section–where I was– sat at the far end away from the door. Our school was driven by the sports programs, so the music and art departments were left to fend for themselves. This part of the school, where I spent most of my time, was a bit musty and dusty, but I loved it all the same.

Becky's eyes scanned the room, searching for a place to sit. As luck would have it, the chair next to me was open. "You saving this," she asked me.

I shook my head, taking in the purple dress she wore.

"Hey," she said, "Your tie kinda matches my dress."

I touched my purplish tie, trying to play it cool. Inside, I was freaking out that this really hot freshman was talking to *me*, the skinny, glasses-wearing, band geek with spikey hair.

While Becky tells a slightly different version of the story, she talked to me A LOT until I finally got the nerve to ask her out. I asked her to go with me to the big bonfire before the first home football game. That first official date marked the beginning of our journey as a couple.

The hallway that led from the band room to the cafeteria was where I'd get my first kiss from Becky, not too many months after that first band class.

I started working for Becky's parents, who were also quite entrepreneurial, the summer after she and I started dating. At the time, the Servant's Centennial General Store was located in a stone building that had served as a makeshift hospital during the Battle of Gettysburg, where the Union General John F. Reynolds was taken after being shot by a sniper.

The cozy, two-story building held a variety of souvenirs, toy rifles, and knick-knacks. Most importantly, the Servants were the 'go-to' spot for authentic, hand-sewn reenactors' gear and accoutrements. Bob and Georgia researched the exact specifications of original Civil War uniforms and had patterns created accordingly. Naturally among the reenacting community, their hand-made goods were a favorite over mass-produced knock offs made overseas.

The Servant's formula of quality products and family-friendly customer service served them well as their business grew and flourished for over twenty-five years with regular customers from all over the world. In fact, when the film *Gettysburg* was shot in town, the Servants provided an authentic wardrobe to thousands of the actors.

Early on, I couldn't imagine how they could be so successful selling souvenirs with basically a few busy summer months a year. Back then, there was no online store, and they relied heavily on two big weekends; the Fourth of July and November 19th, or Remembrance Day, which commemorated the anniversary of President Abraham Lincoln's Gettysburg Address.

Over the next few years, while I worked there, I learned about the importance of volume sales, cost of goods, inventory management, and so much more that opened my eyes and answered my questions. Their unique product mix and healthy margins made it a very profitable business, but what drove people to the Servant's was how Bob and Georgia interacted with people.

What I learned most from the Servants was their willingness to dive in with an idea and take chances. They had fun with their businesses and tried new things. First, there was a doll shop where Georgia created the first Cabbage Patch Birthing Center in Gettysburg. Literally, she simulated Cabbage Patch dolls being born from a cabbage patch. I'm not joking! That shop evolved into a small General Store.

They expanded across the street to a huge General Store and turned the old location into a vintage photoshop called Servant's Olde Tyme Photos (which is still run today by Becky's older brother, Kevin). They added a dress shop and a second General Store location in Harper's Ferry, WV.

Bob and Georgia were always evolving and trying new things, which at the time I thought was crazy, but find myself doing at times now as well.

It's good to stay fresh and try new things as long as the new things don't become a distraction from the core business.

Bob & Georgia Servant	*Servant's Olde Tyme Photos & The Centennial General Store*

Mrs. Servant was definitely the BOSS–her family lovingly nicknamed her The General. What Georgia said, went! They both worked hard and invested everything, and I mean everything, into their businesses. Growing up, Becky's older sister, Gina, basically raised her three younger siblings while Bob and Georgia worked to build the business.

The Servants also made the best of family time, ensuring there was an annual family vacation, at least when business was good. All their kids got involved in activities, with Becky and Angie focused on dance. High expectations abounded, especially when it came to Becky and Angie. Dance lessons evolved into modeling and, later on, even voice lessons. (Have you heard Becky sing? My wife is incredibly talented–but she's most definitely not a singer!)

After high school, I left for college while Becky finished her senior year. We endured being separated for two years while attending different schools before ending up together at Towson State, just outside of Baltimore.

Just like in high school, I got pretty involved in college as well. I played intramural street hockey and ultimate frisbee, joined the PR and Marketing Clubs, tutored in the student advising center, and played pick up games of tennis with Phyllis, who was an 84-year-old classmate in my interpersonal communications class.

I was the only white student at Towson to participate in the Black Student Union. I asked if I could participate in activities to fight against racism and bigotry on campus. In my Junior year, I was crowned TSU Air Hockey Champion (truth be told, I was the only person to show up for the tournament).

When Becky arrived, she quickly became captain of the Towson Dance team, leading them in their first-ever National Competition, where they placed fourth in the country.

I cheered her on from the sidelines at football and basketball games every opportunity I had.

Not long after Becky graduated from college, I decided it was time to take the next step. Having dated continuously for eight years, I thought a marriage proposal would be welcomed by the Servants. I followed the traditional path and asked her father for permission to marry his daughter.

Mr. Servant's blessing came quickly, "BUT"...he said, "You need to get The General's permission."

We sat down at their dining room table, and I slid the ring box across it toward Mrs. Servant. Before I had the chance to open it, she said: "That better be a necklace!" She interrogated me for nearly an hour as Mr. Servant and Becky's sister Angie stood by and witnessed the scene. She said, "Becky is an independent woman who can go in whatever direction she may choose."

At one point, Angie pleaded with her mom to leave me alone. Shortly after, I got The General's blessing.

The days leading up to the big event found me so nervous, not because of the actual proposal, though. I was terrified I might lose the ring, which wasn't anything crazy, but I'd had the ring on layaway for four years, putting all my earnings during high school and college toward it.

I planned for us to enjoy a dinner and dancing cruise on the Potomac in Washington, D.C., followed by a B&B stay at the Inner Harbor in Baltimore. The evening, though chilly, was beautiful, and everything was going as planned.

After dinner, I casually mentioned to Becky that I had hoped to be able to propose to her for her birthday but just couldn't afford a ring yet.

Without hesitation, she said, "That's okay, I'm not ready for that yet anyway."

My stomach dropped, and I began to sweat profusely. I excused myself to the ship's restroom to regroup, double-checking that the ring was still safe on the chain around my neck. I spoke to myself in the mirror, saying, "Dude, she's just trying to make you feel better. She doesn't really mean she wasn't." I swallowed hard. Should I abort the mission? I splashed water on my face, looked myself in the eye, and said, "Hell, no."

I channeled all of the confidence of Paul Rudd in the incredibly hilarious (and highly inappropriate) bathroom scene from *Wanderlust*.

My stomach remained in knots, and my fingers fidgeted with the chain around my neck as I walked back to our table. I had come way too far to back down now, plus I really didn't have the money to set up a night like that anytime soon, so I went for it.

'Let's dance," I said.

She agreed, and we made our way to the small dance floor. I swear I felt like I would either poop my pants or throw up as I eagerly awaited a slow dance to make my move.

The time finally came a few seconds into the first slow dance, and I gently backed away and got down on one knee. I unbuttoned the top button of my shirt, unclasped the chain, and raised the ring in her direction.

She looked at me with an awkward smile and said, "What are you doing down there?"

Either she didn't hear me say, "Will you marry me?" over the music or she really wasn't ready, which would have really been a bummer. I stood up and repeated the question.

She threw her arms around my neck and buried her head on my shoulder. Still, no answer.

By this time, everyone around us realized what was happening and started clapping and cheering. For a little while, I felt like the flight attendant in the exit row asking for a verbal "yes" and then finally got it!

She said, "Yes!"

After eight years of growing up together as high school sweethearts and surviving college, we were engaged.

About six weeks before our wedding, Becky and I enrolled in ballroom classes at Arthur Murray in Towson. Talk about a comedy—I can't dance to save my life, plus I was dealing with a torn ACL in my right knee. We struggled over who would lead. The teacher demonstrated as if I were to lead, but as the long-time dancer and dance teacher, Becky had a hard time relinquishing that role. We moved past stepping on each other's toes and torn ligaments, and I think we had a pretty darn good first dance as husband and wife!

On October 11, 1997, Becky and I became husband and wife. We were married in the magnificent Cathedral of Mary, Our Queen, in Baltimore. It was a big, beautiful wedding with all of the bells and whistles.

Becky was there for me when I needed her most and continues to be for everyone she encounters. Her selflessness and genuine concern for others are what make her so incredibly special.

It wasn't always easy working together 24/7, but once we figured it out, we became even more of a force. We let go of our stubbornness and built upon our strengths and weaknesses. We like to joke that our *power couple* game is strong.

I couldn't have asked for a more perfect partner in business and in life! Becky is my entire heart and soul, my lifeline, and my inspiration.

She challenges and motivates me to be the best Dad I can be, the best business person I can be and the best version of myself. Mrs. Servant was The General, but my Becky is The BOSS!

Becky & Andy, Hawaii 2014

5: A Monster Leaps

"Better late than never but never late is better."
Drake

Becky graduated with a degree in Health Education and initially worked for a large managed care organization, delivering community health programs and information to Baltimore area schools. While the work was good, it drained her and left her feeling unsatisfied.

One day, after yet another tear-filled rant about how much she hated her job, I snapped, "I love you, but you need to stop bitching and do something about it!"

Normally, a remark like this from me shut down our conversations. That time was no different, except Becky took my comment to heart.

A few days later, in May 1999, Becky came home from work and announced, "I've quit my job, and I'm opening a dance studio."

My first thought was, *Great*! No one opens a dance studio in the summer when all the kids are out of school and away on vacations. What I said was, "Go for it."

Inside, my stomach churned as my thoughts ran away from me. We'd just purchased a single-family home in Ellicott City, and my fears over money nearly held us back.

After the initial shock wore off over Becky up and quitting her job, excitement about this new challenge took over. We'd both grown up around family businesses, and Becky had practically lived at a dance studio, but we knew nothing about the ins and outs of running a successful enterprise.

First step... How the hell do you set up a business?

We found an organization called Service Corps of Retired Executives (SCORE), a national non-profit that counsels business owners and entrepreneurs. I visited their Baltimore office and set up three complimentary consultations with local business attorneys. The first one saw us as two green twenty-four and twenty-five-year-olds and literally laughed us out of his office. Next, we met Paul Skalny, and he couldn't have been more encouraging and supportive of our goals. He set us on our path to entrepreneurship, and we've been working together ever since.

The first thing we needed to find was studio space. With our cash extremely limited, we found it difficult to locate something that fell within our means.

Eventually, we discovered Oella Mills, a large, dilapidated warehouse on the Patapsco River. The building dated from 1918 once housed the largest textile mill in the country. The ambiance reminded Becky of a loft-style New York City dance studio, and we loved it—only the rent was outside our budget.

We could have gotten discouraged but instead chose to get creative. We negotiated with the Mills owners, offering to pay a percentage of the dance studio's revenue for the first six months, ramping up meet their full asking rental rate.

Oh—and we wanted the first three months rent waived! Our reasoning was we were excellent risks, we'd be great neighbors to the other tenants, and we would work our butts off to make a go of the studio.

To our surprise and delight, our terms were accepted!

Lack of funds forced creativity, and we worked on a shoestring budget in a one-room studio to get off the ground. Becky's sister Angie and a couple of other friends from Towson agreed to teach classes.

Our "office" was a desk we'd brought from home and put off in the corner. We had no computer, no studio management software, no bookkeeper, and no accounting experience! Our studio was off the beaten path with zero road visibility, and our ballet barres were built from metal pipes I'd purchased at Home Depot. Looking back, we were a little nuts!

I did my best to recall what I learned from the one public relations class I took in college and whipped up a press release. I wrote about this young dance teacher named Becky Funk, who was opening a new dance studio called B.Funk Dance Company that offered hip hop, jazz, tap, and ballet. I sent out the presser, hoping that someone would bite cause we really didn't have extra money to pay for advertising. I even printed quarter-sheet flyers that we put on cars at the local Safeway, Staples, and Bed, Bath & Beyond.

To my shock, journalists called! Two local newspapers wrote articles about Becky and her funky new dance spot. We used that opportunity to host a weekend Open House and included the details in the article.

Becky, Angie, and friends organized a few showcase performances to highlight class offerings. I picked up some punch and cookies. Between twenty and thirty people came through that weekend, and more than half of them signed up on the spot.

WE WERE RICH!

Word spread quickly about the studio as we were the first in the area to offer hip hop classes along with the more traditional dance styles. By the end of the first summer, we had sixty enrolled students, and by the end of the first full year, we had doubled to about 120.

Not having a computer forced me to again get creative to manage customer accounts, I literally used legal-sized paper on a clipboard. With a pencil and ruler, I drew a grid that included family name, month, date paid, and payment type. I feel a mixture of pride and embarrassment that I kept at my paper management process until we had over 100 students. Then, I invested in a desktop computer, and life got much easier.

With the support of her sister and a few other teachers, Becky taught many of the classes. Her workday began when the bell signaled the end of the school day. Becky worked at the studio from five o'clock and, on most nights, taught four classes, including hip hop, jazz, ballet, and creative movement. Angie focused on jazz, contemporary, modern, and musical theater while others taught tap, b-boying, and locking.

I ran the business side of the studio, doing everything from bookkeeping to designing ads to janitorial duties. I was certainly no expert in any of those areas, but we had no choice; we had to make it work with what we had. Oh, and I was still working my full-time job doing development at a non-profit children's charity. Who needs to sleep, right?

God definitely has a sense of humor, especially when it comes to the sleep department. During that first year of B.Funk, Becky and I also learned we were about to become parents. Becky's pregnancy was difficult because she was nauseous and vomiting all day long. Yet, she still taught dance through her eighth month. At nearly nine months along, Becky led her dancers to perform at a charity event for the American Heart Association at the Inner Harbor in Baltimore.

We played a lot of music close to Becky's belly when she was pregnant with our first baby, which we knew was a boy. We decided early on that he would be named Drew Alan after my brother. It was essential to me that Drew knew about Alan and had some connection with him.

I loved cupping my hands around my mouth to create a megaphone and putting it onto her belly and say, *"Hello in therrreee!"* I gave Drew updates on the Orioles and Ravens. We read books and told him stories about his crazy family, especially his Uncle Alan.

As the months passed and Drew's arrival grew near, I felt like my excitement drowned out the fear that had consumed me for many years. For so long, there had been a void in my life, a sense of being alone. I had friends, family, Becky, sports, and work, but losing Alan left me empty.

The hopeless feeling of all of the opportunities and experiences that most siblings enjoy together, and often take for granted, was excruciating at times. Each milestone without Alan reminded me of those ahead of us. There would be no brother getaways, he wasn't in my wedding party, Uncle Alan would be a memorial title my boys would call someone they would never meet.

Many years ago, I decided to celebrate Alan's birthday, March 24, a little differently. On that day, I got a little something for each of the boys to open. It was my small way to keep Alan's memory alive with his nephews.

Speaking of birthdays, Drew's birth meant much more than just a new addition. He brought new life, and he filled a void left by Alan's passing. I'm not overly spiritual, but I believe my connection with Alan was reborn with Drew and each of my sons.

Drew was born in the summer of 2000. Becky stayed with him during the day, going to the studio in the late afternoons. One of my best friends from college and Drew's godfather, William, aka Uncle Busha, helped take care of Drew in the evenings while Becky taught, and I worked the front desk. Becky left for the studio as soon as I got home from my day job, and I followed as soon as William got to our house. We were all essentially going strong (or holding on for dear life) from the time we woke up until the studio closed or until Drew fell asleep.

When Drew was a little older, I would pick him up after work, drive thirty minutes or more to Westminster, or an hour to Gettysburg, to meet my mother-in-law, who watched Drew while we were at the studio. Then we would meet again, or I would drive back to Gettysburg after the studio closed to pick him up. Had *The Walking Dead* been out at that time, we would have been a shoo-in as extras. We nailed the zombie impersonations.

I didn't realize it at that time, but Becky was dealing with a pretty significant case of the baby blues. She gave every ounce of energy she had to the baby and the studio, leaving nothing for herself. Her scarce alone or me-time was devoted to precious sleep. All the while, she brought the same bubbly Becky personality to everyone she encountered. Her students absolutely loved her. I don't know how she did it.

This pattern continued for three years and, finally, in late 2002, I burnt out, Something had to change. Becky and I decided that I either needed to quit my day job and work at B.Funk full-time or hire somebody to manage the studio. Becky and I discussed the options, with our families weighing in, too.

"No one knows the business like you do, Andy," Becky finally said. "We already have 300 students and are growing so fast that there's no time to train someone on all the aspects of what you do for the studio."

We started B.Funk Dance Company on a shoestring budget and certainly didn't come from a wealthy background. I felt terrified about not having a financial safety net that I opted to go part-time rather than outright quitting my job. I lasted about a month before I realized working for someone else was actually hampering our success.

Thankfully, my first full-time job as a freight broker had been a lesson in Risk-Taking 101! Being a risk-taker can't easily be learned: you're either a risk-taker or you aren't. When I interviewed for the freight broker position, I couldn't have been more green. I knew absolutely nothing about trucking or logistics, nor did my friend and former Baltimore Orioles co-worker, Gene Burdette, who interviewed at the same time. The owners at the plastics brokerage saw something in us and took a risk by hiring not one but both of us for jobs where we had no experience. Their business was buying and selling recyclable plastics for pennies on the dollar and building a multi-million dollar company. I didn't always agree with their methods, but they were very savvy entrepreneurs who weren't afraid to bet on themselves. That lesson I took very much to heart and their example led me to that moment where I had my own risk-taking decision to make.

So I cut the cord and left my job. We had to make this work!

And then the panic set in. Had we thought this thing through?

What if we made no money? What was I thinking? Some people call these the "3 a.m. sweats." The problem was I had them all day! The anxiety of being responsible for our business, and our family drove me to ensure B.Funk would be successful. Very successful.

Having job-hopped since college, I remembered The General encouraging me to work for myself. Maybe, I thought, she wasn't so crazy after all. I drew confidence from each of my job experiences, starting with the roller rink and Servant's General Store.

I journaled about all the things I enjoyed from each job, as well as what I didn't. I wrote about my bosses and how they managed, plus how I felt about their styles. I reflected on how I was as an employee and what would have enhanced my skills. My appreciation grew for our parents' and grandparents' humility and work ethic, and what I learned from their examples.

I also fixated on customer service and evaluated every situation I encountered, from Taco Bell to the gas station to the emergency room. No service escaped my dissection!

Van Dyke and Bacon, a shoe store in Ellicott City, forged my deepest appreciation for customer service. Have you ever experienced a real shoe store with knowledgeable staff who fully understands feet? The service provided there blew me away, and it seemed so simple. Exceptional customer service and high-quality products made me a customer for life.

How I felt as a customer, I realized, was what made the difference in every transaction. *There it is*, I thought. That's what will separate our company from everyone else.

While we had so much to learn, I started having fun with this new reality. Which was great because we were just getting started!

6: The Jump Off

"It was all a Dream."
Notorious B.I.G.

So, I went from a "Hell no, I'll never work for myself" attitude to a "This is cool, what's next?" entrepreneur–pretty much overnight.

The studio business doubled in enrollment over the next three years after I began working it full-time, and we moved to a larger, more visible location. We were rolling along fine, but the business itch kicked in hardcore, and I felt the need for more.

It was the summer of 2002 when Becky and her sister, Angie, and I were driving home after the two of them had taken dance classes in New York City. We were brainstorming about how I could leverage my event-planning, marketing, and business skills to create a completely new dance event.

We talked about the things they liked and didn't like from the dance convention industry; what our studio parents liked and didn't like. The dance industry at that time was driven by competitions featuring more traditional genres like Jazz, Ballet, and Tap with a sprinkle of hip hop if you were lucky. We had a passion for hip hop and had seen the positive impact that it had on our growing studio.

We agreed that we were not interested in simply duplicating another competition, even if it was focused solely on hip hop. We had just made the four hours plus drive from Maryland to New York for them to TRAIN, plus they had made numerous trips before for auditions.

Then it hit us: we would take hip hop training to the people! Monsters of HipHop was born.

After lengthy discussions spanning several days, we settled in on an entirely new concept that we thought would take the dance industry by storm. We had no idea then just how much it really would. Excitement and anticipation grew as we jumped in and got to work.

We immediately threw out artists' names like Michael and Janet Jackson, Prince, Mariah Carey, Justin Timberlake, Britney Spears, Madonna, and more. They were some of the biggest artists of the time, and we wanted to get to the choreographers behind their moves. That was our move.

There was a bit of reluctance on Becky and Angie's part in terms of our ability to find and then get those people to work with us. After all, we had no industry contacts and no real experience, not to mention a brand new idea that was somewhat risky. The studio business was going well, but we didn't have a stash of disposable cash or a wealthy family to fund our fantasy event. Nonetheless, we persisted.

I took the girls' reticence as a bit of a challenge. "Let's get the world's top ten hip hop choreographers together in one place and invite people from all over to come train with them."

Back home, I searched online for the name of Janet Jackson's choreographer and other well-known artists' choreographers. I assembled a list and started making calls.

I expanded my search criterion to include people instrumental in the foundation of the hip hop movement. That's when I discovered Rennie Harris Pure Movement in Philadelphia. Clearly, they were doing incredible work in the field of hip hop education, so I trekked up Interstate 95 to meet with them. I wanted to share our hip hop convention idea with them. Along the way, I met with Terry Wright, Raphael Xavier, and Moncel Durden, all of whom ultimately shared their extensive knowledge at the first Monsters' event.

One of the calls I made was to a Los Angeles-based talent agency,

McDonald Selznick & Associates. To my surprise, Julie McDonald took my call. I explained our hip hop dance convention concept, asking, "Who are the most respected choreographers you represent?"

Julie agreed to send me resumes along with the fees to have them appear in person for our convention–talk about sticker shock! We had no clue what rates ought to be for this kind of event and did little to no negotiation. Interestingly, many of the choreographers had never taught in a convention setting.

Monsters had no history, had never produced a large scale dance event like the one we were proposing, and no one knew who Becky and Andy Funk were outside of Gettysburg, Towson, or Ellicott City, Maryland. So, we paid their rates and unknowingly set a new bar for convention pay. While we may have overpaid for the first event, we also successfully got TEN of the TOP choreographers in the world to agree to our crazy idea. Mission accomplished!

We booked the Philadelphia Convention Center for April 2003. We picked Philly because of its proximity to NYC and Baltimore, and it was already home to three of the teachers. My stomach sank when I saw the cost to have the top talent for our event–and sank further once I'd signed the convention center contract. In for a penny, in for a pound, I thought. To just break even, we needed 200 registrants. All our money was tied to that first event, and everything rested on it being successful.

Let me set the stage. In 2003, Facebook was brand new and only available to a few college kids. Social media didn't exist. There were no Instagram, Twitter, Dropbox, no Google, no iTunes, and no Amazon. There was no YouTube. You likely had Hotmail or Yahoo or AOL to deliver your email. Instant messenger was AOL's IM (do you remember your handle?). Good ole snail mail did the trick.

Becky taught at B.Funk and helped shape Monsters while Angie and I tackled the research. We logged onto dance.net, really the only dancer-related website back then, to seek out information about dance studios offering hip hop instruction.

We spent hours on superpages.com looking for hip hop dance educators and studios and copied down all the names and addresses we could find. We ended up with a list of about 1,200 names up and down the east coast, from Boston to Florida. That resulted in our first mailing.

I traveled back and forth to New York City, setting up a table at the Broadway Dance Center, handing out flyers and telling everyone who would listen that there would be a hip hop dance convention in Philadelphia.

"The top ten choreographers will teach," I said. "The biggest names in the industry."

"Is it a show?" one girl asked (so did about a hundred others).

Over and over, I explained the format.

The responses ranged from "That's cool" to "Hmmm. Interesting." I existed on adrenaline and coffee, trying not to let my perception of their interest (or lack thereof) discourage me.

I understood their lack of faith. At most dance conventions, dancers would spend a weekend taking jazz, tap, contemporary, or ballet classes. Yet, they might only get one sixty-minute class of hip hop. They were also accustomed to the convention weekend being driven by hours of competition dancing and trophies. And here we were telling everyone that an entire weekend would be devoted to training and networking with the best hip hop names in the world. There were more than a few doubtful laughs when I delivered my pitch.

Right from the very beginning, we wanted to ensure that our event would be a family-friendly experience where everyone who participated felt welcomed and supported. Our core values were embedded in every decision, and it showed. We felt an obligation to dispel the negative connotation some people associate with hip hop because we knew the hip hop dance community was incredibly supportive and accepting.

That first event was bootstrapped. Thank goodness for our families and friends–without them, none of that life-changing event would have worked. Everyone pitched in and did anything we asked. In fact, the photo on the cover of this book shows both my grandmothers and my parents, holding Drew and baby Cooper, folding Monsters of HipHop merchandise on our kitchen table. Love was folded into every one of those hoodies!

Every day, I jumped up to get the mail as soon as I heard the postal worker drive off, hoping (and praying) for new registrations to be in our box. I obsessed over receiving the mail so much that sometimes I forgot what day it was and would check on Sunday. Even though I'm not the dancer in our family, I did a happy dance every time a registration envelope arrived!

I did have one brief foray into a dance class, but it didn't last long as I got kicked out of class for questioning the teacher. Becky and I went to see Savion Glover in the incredible show *Bring in 'da Noise, Bring in 'da Funk*. My mind was blown, and the percussionist in me could not sit still, rather I could not keep my hands still. Becky encouraged me to take the adult tap class at the studio, and I reluctantly agreed.

I heard (in my head) different beats than MY WIFE, who was teaching in our tap class. Needless to say, she didn't appreciate it when I would suggest hitting additional beats. Clearly, my musicality was just on a higher level. I tried one more year of tap with Ms. JR, and she was more forgiving, but I also realized that I was better suited for the front or back of the house as opposed to on stage.

Anyway, Angie and I tracked every paper registration form and celebrated when they arrived. We needed about 200 registrations to break even and sold just shy of 300 at 291 for our first event in Philadelphia.

We created a handbook that outlined everyone's schedule, when and where to be, what to wear, who was responsible for escorting choreographers from class to class. I recently found the original staff handbook Angie and I created for that first event, its bright yellow cover dusty from sitting on a basement shelf.

The pages included detailed timelines for each day. We outlined our Code of Conduct: respectful, helpful, and patient. While I don't recall all the details, the schedule listed a "mandatory walkthrough" of the Convention Center on Friday, April 11, 2003, promptly at 8 p.m.

It's funny to look back and realize how much forethought went into that first convention, especially since we'd never run one before. Every internship, every job experience, and, of course, growing up around family businesses went into our every move.

I have to say that our first event was something to behold!

I remember walking into the convention center incredibly nervous but oddly excited that the time had finally come to pull off our grand plan. I felt like this was our Super Bowl. We had customers taking a chance on us, and we had to deliver! I felt confident but wanted to make sure that we made good on the hype of what we promised.

I'm not sure that I ever slowed to take a breath before walking in to kick off the event. We rolled from one task to another by the seat of our pants from the second we arrived at the Convention Center, where I learned that it was a Union facility.

That meant I could not have our staff assist with moving in our equipment and materials. As the point of contact, I was the only one who could do the load in without having to hire the convention center staff.

I took a deep breath and spent the next several hours making trip after trip to our cars using a flatbed cart to load everything into place. Once everything was in the venue, our staff could take over to help set up. That was the first reality check, but we adapted and made the best of a surprising situation (I'd like to say it was the last surprise, but it wasn't).

Choreographers arrived in Philadelphia at different times, with some flying in from Los Angeles, and others driving in from New York. I picked each of the choreographers up who flew into Philadelphia International. For most of them, that was the first time they'd met us, which was both exciting and nerve-racking as we wanted to make a good first impression. I channeled my experience of giving Camden Yards tours to Major League Baseball executives from around the country. While I didn't go as far as holding up a sign with their names scrawled on it, I did make sure to wear my Monsters of HipHop hoodie so they would recognize me.

Giving tours to a group of twenty or thirty people was no big deal for me, but standing on stage alongside celebrities in front of a hundred or so people who were all taking a chance on us felt terrifying. I'd like to think that I sounded coherent and didn't make a fool of myself as I welcomed everyone to the first Monsters event. I recall looking out into the room but couldn't tell you what I said. I did feel a tremendous sense of relief when the music started for the first time in the Advanced room. Our event was off and running, and there was no turning back. To this day, I can feel the energy and excitement while Lil Kim's *The Jump Off* filled the room.

By the time our first-ever event kicked off, we knew we'd already exceeded expectations, and began thinking about future events. We wanted the choreographers to have a great experience so they'd return, so we gave them SWAG bags full of snacks and Monsters gear, and because the hotel rooms were off-site from the convention center, we had designated staff to escort them and get them whatever they needed. We treated them to dinner and paid them more than they had ever been paid for teaching. We went above and beyond, treating them like the artists they were—something a lot of hip hop dancers and choreographers weren't used to.

Top hip hop choreographers joined us as teachers for the event, and they deserve credit for believing in our vision from the start: Fatima Robinson, Travis Payne, Jermaine Browne, Rhapsody James, Napoleon Dumo, Brian Friedman, Shawnette Heard, Terry Wright, Raphael Xavier, and Moncel Durden.

We learned early on the difference between an incredibly creative choreographer and a naturally gifted teacher. Teaching a room full of hundreds of aspiring dancers requires a much different skill set than working one on one with the likes of Janet Jackson or Britney Spears in a studio.

I honestly feel like there was a sense of nervousness on the choreographers' parts as well, especially from those who had not taught in a convention setting before. Some asked questions like, "will there be mirrors," while others fumbled with which direction to face while teaching. These were the biggest names in the business, but not all of them were comfortable in that setting. Like us, they adapted to the situation and made it work just fine.

While it was hectic and I felt like a sweaty mess most of the weekend, there were special moments with people that have stayed with me to this day.

A few months before the event in Philadephia, I answered a phone call from a well-spoken young man inquiring about Monsters.

He said, "Hi, my name is Tony Testa, and I'm calling from Fort Collins, Colorado, with a few questions about Monsters of HipHop taking place at the Pennsylvania Convention Center this April."

Our conversation was so memorable that when I saw a young man approaching me with a confident, artistic stroll, arm extended for a courteous handshake, I just knew it was Mr. Testa. Tony would become a cast member in our inaugural Monsters Show in Los Angeles in 2005 and the first alumni to join our faculty to teach a few years later.

Laura Edwards, who attended the first event, also performed in the inaugural Monsters Show and joined our faculty shortly after that. In 2015, she bought B.Funk from us, and we knew she was the perfect person to take over our first business. It was her presence and personality at the first Monsters event that stood out to Becky in particular, and she's been stuck with us ever since.

We felt we had everything under control, though, in hindsight, we made loads of mistakes. For example, someone asked me where to find water. I told them about a little shop around the corner.

"You don't have water," he said, incredulous at our gaffe.

The convention center was great. Shortly after my harried request for water stations, the center staff had them set up, and no one died of thirst. Problem solved!

The students loved the convention, and their families did, too. The choreographers had a total blast. The energy, the environment, the entire family-friendly experience. It felt like magic.

As the Philadelphia event wound down, I found myself riding the escalator with Brian Friedman, one of the choreographers. He said, "So, when's the next one?"

The next one? I thought. Shoot, we hadn't gotten that far. I said, "Oh yeah, we're working on it. We wanted to see how this one went first."

Brian looked at me and said, "You've got to do this."

After we returned home from Philadelphia, I felt both thoroughly exhausted and a powerful sense of accomplishment. We'd really done it! Those feelings didn't last long as I quickly moved to anticipation for what needed to happen next.

Customers loved the convention and wanted more—and we wanted to give it to them. We dove deep into research and planning modes, back at it again on dance.net to sort out which cities to attend.

Post-Philly, we crunched data and discovered that we'd had attendees from thirteen states! We used this information to determine where we would go next, choosing major cities where we could find the largest number of studios or crews advertising hip hop classes.

I didn't do many site visits, but the first one I made was to Oakland, California, to see my new friend Kim Battiste, who had called and emailed every month for about six months before our first event begging us to bring Monsters to Oakland, California.

Within a month and a half after the inaugural event, I had booked a seven-city nationwide tour: San Francisco, Denver, Seattle, Orlando, Chicago, Dallas, and East Brunswick, New Jersey. We shifted from Philadelphia to New Jersey to be closer to New York City and also so we could move into a hotel instead of the convention center.

Again, this was new territory, with me learning on the fly just like my first full-time job as a freight broker, which I knew nothing about. So, booking a nationally touring dance convention, committing tens of thousands of dollars that we did not have, I felt like this was just another leap of faith.

We jumped and didn't look back.

7: Welcome to the Show

"My life is one big rhyme, and I try to scheme through it."
Common

A year or so after our first event in Philly, we reflected on what made Monsters unique and brainstormed ways to stay ahead of the game and provide even more opportunities for our customers. After the completion of our 2003/2004 tour, we saw a need to further support dancers as they ventured into dance careers.

Competition was not our lane and also not the big break that dancers needed, but we knew there had to be more. Becky always loved theater and wanted to do a Broadway-style hip hop show, so with a little more discussion, The Monsters Show was born.

Here's how it worked: at each tour stop, we held videotaped auditions for dancers to have a chance to perform at a live show to be held in Los Angeles at the conclusion of our tour. Our faculty reviewed the footage and nominated sixteen of the most exceptional dancers.

These chosen few traveled to Los Angeles and jumped into some of the most intense training with the world's top choreographers that they would ever experience–they would be seen by the industry's top agents.

Once again, we knew this was a great idea, but had no idea how we would pull it off, with whom, where, and WITH WHAT MONEY?! We took a huge financial risk hoping that people would want to buy tickets.

This might be a good time to mention that my all-time favorite movie is the 1989 film *Field of Dreams*. Iowa farmer Ray Kinsella hears voices telling him, "If you build it, they will come." He plows down his cornfields and builds a baseball field. I know it was just Hollywood, but I love that he built that field on faith—and was rewarded when fans came. We did the same with The Monsters Show and hoped that people would come.

At the same time that I was planning the 2004-2005 tour, I began searching for a theater in Los Angeles and settled on North Hollywood, which was the heart of the dance community.

I had no idea what to expect and completely guessed on what size theatre to book, how many shows to do, how to price tickets, and so much more. We had previously produced dance recitals with an audience of 800-1,000 people, but this was an entirely different concept. So, in the heart of the entertainment capital of the world, we once again started from scratch, leveraging our faculty and a few agency contacts.

I booked the 375-seat El Portal Theatre on Lankershim Boulevard in North Hollywood, California, for a week in August 2005. The El Portal Theatre was a fixture in North Hollywood—or NOHO, as it's called by the locals—was the hub of the dance community. It was ambitious to think we could sell out two shows for that first-ever show, Not only did we do just that, we added and filled a matinee as well!

The First Sold Out Monsters Show at the
El Portal Theatre

We launched the tour along with news of this new opportunity and then got to work to figure out how to pull it off.

Our faculty loved the idea, too, but we needed more help than encouragement. We knew that it had to be more than a showcase and not just a glorified dance recital. While we had a vision of the framework, we weren't the creative directors or choreographers who would make the magic happen.

Two in the faculty stepped up and volunteered to write a treatment and help coordinate the event. Husband and wife duo, Tabitha and Napoleon Dumo (known professionally as Nappytabs), taught with us since the beginning. They were still relatively young in terms of the industry with very few credits, but they jumped right in and assembled an awesome crew to assist.

When it came time to create the show's program, I suggested listing Tabitha and Napoleon as "directors," which they were reluctant to claim because they didn't want to step on other choreographers' toes. I reminded them that they had stepped up, taking the creative lead, and I felt they deserved the title. They went on to direct the next several Monsters' shows, experimenting with concepts and building what has become a brilliant career.

When we arrived in Los Angeles to kick off the inaugural show, all of the feelings I'd had at that first Philadelphia event resurfaced—nerves, excitement, and an overwhelming desire to impress and entertain. We'd put ourselves and our brand out there again, this time in the heart of the dance industry and the entertainment capital of the world! To say we were stressed would be an understatement. Even more so, we stood to lose money—a lot of it—that we couldn't afford to lose, but we gambled that people would buy tickets to the event.

We sold out our first three shows at the El Portal theatre in North Hollywood that year, and our signature event took hold.

That first cast of dancers really didn't know what they were getting themselves into, and, to be honest, we didn't fully know either. We certainly didn't know then that what we were creating would transform an entire industry.

I recently attended a business presentation by world-renowned community impact leader Jamie McDonald. In her presentation about Big ideas, she showed a picture of a man standing toward the top of a mountain with the caption "Be sure to stop and look back down the mountain!" The lesson was that even though he still had a long way to go, he took the time to stop and appreciate how far he had come.

That lesson reminded me of the first time I stopped to acknowledge how special and transformative The Monsters Show really was. We'd been doing the show for several years when a few cast members' words and thank you cards touched me so deeply that I stopped for a moment to reflect on what we had done. At that moment, I was literally moved to tears. I acknowledge how proud I am of this particular business decision and the risks we took early on.

Before each show, I gather the entire cast to remind them how far they've come and tell them that the show is their time to let go, have fun, and entertain. I also take a moment to offer my thanks for allowing me to honor my brother Alan. I briefly share his story about how he died at nineteen years old and that everything I do, including the Monsters' Show, is to make a difference and honor his legacy. I share how hard he fought and that his time was cut short. If I can convince one of those kids to go on and make the best of their lives, then I was successful.

For the dancers who perform in the Monsters Show, it can be the catalyst to launch their career if they continue to push forward. Like the man who turned around to appreciate his journey to that point on the mountain, they also realize (if we've taught them well enough) that their journey has just begun.

I'll never forget the 2007 Monsters Show titled *Inspirations*. Well-known producer Nigel Lythgoe of *So You Think You Can Dance* fame attended the show. He was supposed to come with a guest but arrived alone.

Napoleon said to me, "Funk, you need to sit with Nigel."

I walked up and introduced myself and walked Nigel to his seat. "May I join you?" I asked, and he couldn't have been nicer in welcoming me to do so.

Nigel and I chatted about how the history of Monsters and the evolution of The Monsters Show. I explained about the auditions at our conventions, the nominations process, yadda yadda yadda. I emphasized that the entire production had come together in ten days from the time the cast met one another to tonight's show. Throughout the show, he asked questions about each choreographer and their pieces, about our special guests, about the directors, and so on. He asked to meet Tabitha and Napoleon, so during intermission, we made our way to the control booth, where Nigel applauded them and the entire show. What an incredibly cool moment for all of us!

After intermission, we returned to our seats for the second act. In my excitement, I had forgotten that we had worked in a comedic spoof of *So You Think You Can Dance,* featuring the late Andre Fuentes who did a brilliant portrayal in drag of a fictional host, Kitty Cat Seacrest.

The lights came down as the opening track from the television show set the scene. My stomach sank, and I began to sweat a little. What if Nigel didn't think it was funny? Worse, what if he was offended? Fortunately, he loved it, and his laughter set my mind at ease. After the show, he expressed his gratitude for our hospitality and complimented the dancers before taking his leave.

He has since attended multiple shows, offering terrific reviews, saying that the Monsters Show was "amazing, immersive, and enthralling." A huge highlight was receiving a rave review from LA Times dance critic Debra Levine who called the Monsters Show "Infectious, crazy, fun and flawlessly executed."

Since then, The Monsters' Show has been the catalyst to some of the industry's biggest success stories. The man behind Beyonce's moves in her iconic *Single Ladies* video, JaQuel Knight, got his big break two weeks after performing in The Monsters Show. Nick DeMoura, choreographer and creative director for stars like Justin Bieber and Ariana Grande, traveled from Massachusetts to LA on a one-way flight to be an alternate in the 2006 Monsters Show.

Halfway through show rehearsals, I spoke with Nick about his goals and plans, and he made the decision to stay in Los Angeles, worked at a California Pizza Kitchen, and grinded on his own to get where he is today. These and countless other stories like them are what make The Monsters' Show the most anticipated live dance show in our industry.

The Monsters' Show is like no other in that the process rivals that of a professional tour. For two weeks, the cast is pushed to their limits mentally and physically to create an hour and a half show. It's not uncommon for rehearsals to go for twenty hours a day on back-to-back-to-back days. Our faculty pours their hearts and soul into this show because they know what it will do for these kids. They are dream fulfillers and career launchers.

Fifteen years in, people now attend Monsters from all over the world to train with our influential faculty and for the chance to be cast in The Monsters Show. Monsters' cast members have come from Japan, Canada, Mexico, Slovenia, Australia, Poland, the United Kingdom, and Ireland–to name a few.

As hip hop has grown in popularity and more studios began offering instruction at younger ages, we have seen the talent get younger and younger to the point that we decided to add a Kids' Cast to the show. Now, it's hard to find a tour, commercial, television, or awards show that doesn't have at least one Monsters' alumni. To name a few: on Taylor Swift's Reputation Tour, six of about fifteen dancers were all Monsters Show kids; two danced on the same tour with Camilla Cabello; three others were in Janet Jackson's Vegas Show; four in Gwen Stefani's Vegas Show; and a couple each with Chris Brown and Jennifer Lopez. Monsters trained dancers are everywhere!

We quickly saw the impact that The Monsters Show had on the dancers. Little did we know, it also cultivated aspiring choreographers as well.

For example, JaQuel Knight was selected as part of the 2008 Monsters Show...but not initially. That was one of the most heated selection meetings in history! Two well-known choreographers had differing opinions on his selection, and, in the heat of the moment, there erupted a shouting match, and several faculty members walked out.

At the end of the night, JaQuel was on the outside looking in. It wasn't until our Orlando finale convention when JaQuel blew everyone away in every class that Becky spoke to the faculty and urged them to add him to the cast.

Since then, JaQuel has gone on to be named to *Forbes* 30-Under-30 List, an achievement that is more difficult than being accepted into Stanford or Harvard.

Becky with Jake Landgrebe at the Taylor Swift Concert

That same year's show included a little known dancer from New Zealand named Parris Goebel, who has gone on to become one of the most recognized and celebrated choreographers in the world. Additionally, award-winning singer/songwriter, Victoria Monet, joined that same cast.

Since performing in the 2007 Monsters Show, Sean Bankhead has also taken the entertainment world by storm. He is the man behind Missy Elliott, Normani, Fifth Harmony, and tons more and one of the most genuine people you'll ever meet.

We could not be prouder to have witnessed their rise and been a small part of their journey along with hundreds of others. Some of the best moments are when we have an opportunity to see "our kids" doing what they love. Watching our alumni perform in front of sold-out audiences, waving to us from the stage, is the most amazing feeling.

While we've learned to take the time to "stop and look back down the mountain" around show time each year, one thing we have not really gotten comfortable with is sharing how amazing the program really is. We've never been the type to shout our own praises, so when Rhapsody, who has been with us since day one, directed the 15th Anniversary Monsters Show, it pushed us way out of our comfort zone.

Andy with Director Rhapsody James at the 15th Anniversary Show

Rhapsody told our story in the most incredible and meaningful way, gathering interviews, and personal stories from family, faculty, and numerous dancers. Watching the Show from the audience and hearing the stories up close and personal from people who claimed that we changed or even saved their lives brought me to tears. Rhapsody and so many others shared stories of community, family, and realness that Monsters fosters. In many ways, her push in that show contributed to me picking up and finishing this book. This was step one in improving our self-promotion.

Success Breeds Success. This became evident several years into producing The Show.

One downside of working with the world's top choreographers is that they often get pulled away for whichever artist they're working with. In the early days, there were a few occasions talent would get called in the middle of show rehearsals. That's when we recognized how many of our show alumni were also becoming talented choreographers, so we gave them a chance to show what they could do in The Monsters Show.

Alumni have created some of the most incredible pieces, and, in 2019, The Monsters' Show concept was created and directed by two alumni for the first time, Mel Charlot and Robert Green. While the 2011 show was entitled, "Full Circle," the 2019 show truly was a full circle experience, not to mention an extremely rewarding one. I witnessed Mel grow as a Director/ Mentor learning from Rhapsody on the previous three shows. And with Robert, it was an incredible moment as I recalled his early days attending Monsters with his Mom. I had no idea until years later, but Robert and his Mom slept in their car during Monsters weekends and ate peanut butter and jelly sandwiches to get through.

This new found choreography talent presented another opportunity, and one we were determined to figure out what to do with. We still had the top choreographers in the industry, but fresh faces kept coming onto the scene with a passion and desire to teach.

Around the same time, we received many requests to produce a hip hop competition, something we never intended to do as our mission was primarily focused on training and education, not trophies and medals.

So, we combined the ingredients in front of us and created an entirely new event called Monsters AList. Initially, the "A" in AList stood for Alumni as all of the faculty teaching at the AList events would be Monsters Show alumni. Honestly, I think we got too cute with the thought process and eventually gave up trying to explain the origin.

 AList was designed to be different from typical conventions. Not only did it focus solely on hip hop and commercial dance, but we drew the line at giving trophies to those dancers who came in first, second, or third. In real life, not everyone gets a trophy and, in my humble opinion, giving everyone trophies has backfired–and at least in the dance industry, I know it has.

I've spoken with countless dance moms and dads whose children have won every title and trophy there is to win, but when they moved to L.A. to dance professionally, they weren't ready and got eaten alive. Professional dance is NOT an easy business, especially without mental toughness, to go along with the talent. Oh, by the way, you have to be the right height, have the right hair color, or been in the right place at the right time, or (I hate to say it) had a high enough social media "Followers" (but this soapbox is for a different book, so don't get me started).

The last thing I want is one of our attendees to up and move to L.A., have their dreams crushed, and return home with their tails between their legs. Rather, I want them to chase their dreams and do so with their eyes open, prepared for the inevitable challenges they'll face.

AList combines the best of what people have come to love about Monsters with new amazing choreographers and the ability to compete in the style they love. Basically, it's Monsters Plus! One unique AList feature is the A-Game Agency Award, which we've built upon using our long-standing relationships in L.A. This introduction has led to numerous agency contracts.

What started largely on a dare, has become one of the most transformative companies in the entire dance industry.

Family
Photos

Faculty Photos

**Show
Photos**

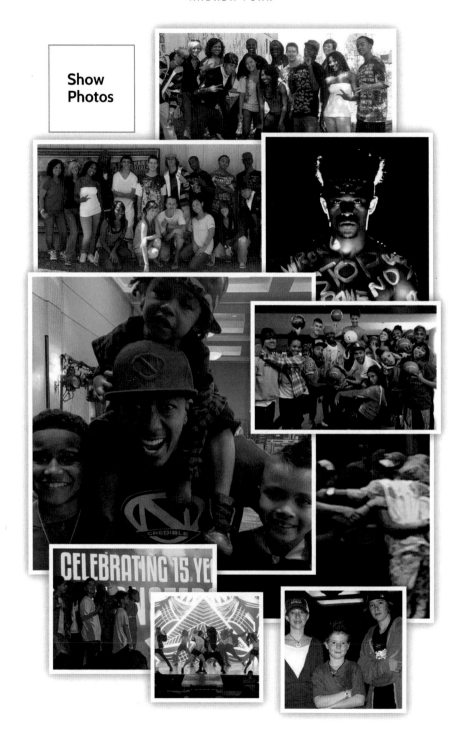

Alumni Photos

**Staff
Photos**

8: Faith and Fear

"Next time you see a brother down, stop and pick him up,
cause you might be the next one stuck."
Grand Puba

It's easy to stay in faith when things are going well. But when you're tested on multiple fronts, trusting that everything will work out can be harder.

In early 2000, my uncle and I carried my Dad from his bed to the car to get him to the hospital. He had been dealing with severe Rheumatoid Arthritis for many years, but it had flared up so badly that he couldn't get himself out of bed. After lengthy stays in Hershey and at Johns Hopkins in Baltimore, he started to improve and eventually got back on his feet, and once again, the RA was under control.

Dad was better, we had a successful recital to wrap up our first year in the studio business, and our son, Drew, was born in July. Life was good!

Then, on August 16, 2000, I received a phone call from Becky. I was working full-time for the Orioles at Gallery E, a sports art gallery in the Warehouse at Camden Yards. My Mom had been involved in an accident and was being flown to York Hospital.

Before I had a chance to ask anything, Becky said she was on her way to pick me up to take me to the hospital. Immediately, questions flooded my mind. Why couldn't I drive myself there? Why was Mom being flown to York instead of driven to the local hospital in Gettysburg? What wasn't Becky telling me? My mind raced through every possible terrible outcome.

On the way to the hospital, I tried to get more information from Becky, but it was evident that either she didn't know much or just wasn't telling me. All I knew was my mom had been hit by a Mack truck, and the Jaws of Life were used to cut her mangled Nissan Altima apart to rescue her. I felt absolutely terrified.

Upon our arrival at the hospital, we were met by the doctor who first saw my mom. He said that if I believed in miracles, my mom had just experienced one. After being pushed the length of two football fields by a Mack truck, she escaped with only a broken leg and crushed forearm. She was lucky to be alive.

Mom's Nissan Altima after her Accident

Over the next several months, Mom went through intense rehab and physical therapy. Unfortunately, I don't remember being there to help her or cheer her on as much as I probably should have. I know we visited, but living a little over an hour away, it was difficult to get there as much as I would have liked. We had an infant at home, a growing business, and I was still working a full-time job. I didn't have the luxury of taking off much time as I would have liked. Knowing what I know

now, I wish I would have been more present for my parents during that time.

I still had lessons to learn—and most of them the hard way.

In January 2008, I had embarked on a road trip to the Carolinas with Gene Burdette, who was working with us to visit studios and promote Monsters in the southeast. It was early evening when I received a phone call from Drew on Becky's phone. He told me that Becky's Mom, Georgia, had suffered a heart attack. At that point, all they knew was that paramedics tried CPR for over twenty minutes before getting her heart to beat. They expected severe brain damage and the family was faced with incomprehensible decision to stop life support.

Gene and I diverted to the closest airport where I got on the next available flight home, and he continued on the trip. This is something that has happened numerous times over the years, and we are incredibly grateful that we have such an amazing staff who always has our backs! And it was not only Monsters staff. Becky's crew at the studio stepped in so that Becky could be with her family as long as needed.

Miraculously, Georgia pulled through but suffered short term memory loss, which made the next several years quite a challenge for the family.

In 2009, we lost both Grandma and PapPap Kerrigan to cancer, and shortly after, I convinced myself that I could recondition my body to need less sleep. For years, I'd been accustomed to working long hours so that I could keep up and be present as much as possible with our kids. I always had more work to do.

For about ten days leading up to our Chicago convention, I got the kids to sleep and then stayed up working until about 2:00 a.m., would sleep for about four hours, and then get up at 6:00 a.m. to start all over. This schedule rolled into Chicago, and I felt like I was doing great UNTIL I arrived home and crashed hard. Sickness hit, and I couldn't get out of bed for several days. I realized that I couldn't keep the pace, and something had to give, yet somehow I persisted.

By 2011, the strain of running two businesses together, raising three active sons, and working nonstop started to show. Pressure built up. Our marriage faltered because we weren't focused on it. We'd been together so long that we kind of took our relationship for granted. Our schedules were opposite, and it felt like we were ships passing in the night.

We always found a way to work things out, but it was definitely not smooth sailing, and it was only just beginning. I had felt the need for help for some time and finally took the leap to hire our second full-time employee, which was both stressful and a huge relief.

On top of everything else, Becky was exhausted to the point where she had to take naps—plural—to get through the day. She kept telling me, "I don't understand why I'm so tired. It feels like I'm watching my life through a foggy window."

Years before, Becky's doctor had prescribed for her depression medication when she experienced similar challenges. All I knew was she wasn't herself. Moodiness set in, and I wondered if she might be depressed again. She said she wasn't, but it would have been totally understandable if she had been.

God forgive me, I also thought, "She's just lazy." Through a haze of my own exhaustion, I picked up the slack as best I could with the family responsibilities, the studio, and Monsters.

Our lives were working and resentment built. The few conversations we had typically ended in an argument. Becky didn't feel understood, and I felt put upon. We started couples counseling.

Even so, Becky kept insisting something else was wrong. But the doctors she visited all said the same thing, "This is normal. You're running two businesses, you have three kids. You're getting older."

She didn't feel like anyone was listening to her. "This isn't normal for me," she insisted. And even began questioning her sanity.

Doctors know best, so we did ours by soldiering on as best we could—until Becky's body failed.

We'd taken our kids to a Monster Truck Rally at the Baltimore Arena.

The metallic sounds of trucks grinding away were enough to give Becky an excruciating headache. We got home around ten that night.

"I really don't feel well. My head doesn't feel right," she said, climbing the stairs to our bedroom. "I feel numb." As she spoke, she folded into herself, sliding down onto the floor.

I called our neighbors, the Groves, who rushed over to stay with the boys, and then I somehow got Becky to the car. We rushed to the emergency room at Howard County General Hospital.

"We'll keep her overnight," said the neurologist, who finally saw us. "Her symptoms are classic for migraines. To be sure, tomorrow, we'll run an MRI and some additional tests."

We both felt a sense of relief at finally having some answers. Migraines could be easily treated.

The next day, I stayed at the hospital as we waited for Becky to be discharged. The clock inched toward school dismissal time. "Am I cool to leave to go pick up the kids?" I asked, hoping that might hurry the discharge process.

The doctor assured me that I could leave and that Becky would be ready to go once I returned.

Ten minutes later, my cell phone rang. It was Becky. She's sobbing hysterically.

Turns out that the doctor came back just after I'd left and said to Becky, "I'm sorry. I didn't fully read the neurology report. You have Multiple Sclerosis."

I felt my cheeks burn with anger as fear fluttered in my stomach. I was furious that a doctor could display such an appalling lack of empathy. I mean, who casually tosses out bad news like it was candy? I tried to remain calm and reassuring on the phone, but as soon as I hung up, I lost it as well. My stomach sank with a feeling of utter helplessness and disbelief.

I turned the car around and rushed back to the hospital. Our neighbors once again saved the day by picking up and caring for our sons until my parents could arrive from Gettysburg.

Testing ensued, and information flooded in. Steroids. Flare-ups. Auto-immune disorders. Neurology. Johns Hopkins. It was all a blur. Fear of "what does this mean" for a dancer and a teacher was unspoken between us.

The boys' school community rallied and offered support that was wonderful but awkward at the same time. We were used to providing the support, so when they asked to deliver meals to the boys and me while Becky was in the hospital, we initially declined.

"It's as much for us as it is for you guys," they said, so we reluctantly accepted.

The dance studio families asked to set up a team for the local Multiple Sclerosis Walk in Becky's honor. It was all too much at the time, but so appreciated now when we look back upon the outpouring of support. In many ways, it reminded me of the support my parents received when my brother was sick.

Becky said, "I felt such relief at knowing I wasn't crazy. Or lazy."

Underlying her exhaustion and our marital challenges had been this dormant health issue. I felt like a jerk.

It was then that we really appreciated the strength of our commitments: to each other, our family, and our businesses. Funny how clarity follows a crisis.

And while 2011 wasn't necessarily the best year of our lives—we'd also lost Grandma Funk—there were some bright spots, and ultimately it was the turning point we needed. We did have the privilege of being part of ABC's *Extreme Makeover Home Edition* with choreographers Laura Edwards, Nick DeMoura, Ian Eastwood, and Lyle Beniga, who provided dance classes as part of the episode.

I'd like to tell you that the event went as planned, but it didn't. Hurricane Irene rampaged through Maryland, leaving us without power on the weekend ABC's crew and 150 dancers arrived to shoot the show.

We made the event happen, with one boom box running on a

generator and no air conditioning. It was blazing hot, but everyone who attended had a positive, memorable experience. It was nice to hear how professional and smooth our operation was, despite having just come through a hurricane.

By then, Becky was ready to give up the studio. I struggled with the idea of losing that steady stream of income. The recession of 2008 wasn't too far in the rear view mirror, and Monsters had a full-time staff now, for whom we paid salary and benefits. Putting everything on the line scared the crap out of me. One thing that gave me comfort was knowing that we had gone through the worst of times and made it through. We were confident in our product, in ourselves, and our ability and drive to persevere. After producing a successful (and quite memorable) event in the aftermath of a hurricane, we knew that whatever came at us next, our problem-solving skills would carry us through. Even more, we trusted in our community! *BIG TRUSS! (Let's Go, Ravens!)*

Had we not had the blessing of Becky's diagnosis, I know for sure we'd have done things differently. We had missed out on being fully present with our children and allowing others to shine. We chose to step back from working in our businesses and work on them instead. This meant we had to hire help for the day-to-day...and take a hard look at where and how we wanted to spend our time.

The truth was that Becky's health was significantly impacted by the stress of running the dance studio. We explored the idea of selling outright, but nothing worked out.

Our breaking point came late in 2014 when Becky had an M.S. flare-up and was bedridden for a while. Some ridiculous parent-teacher drama erupted at the studio, and the anxiety and stress Becky felt exacerbated her symptoms. I was actually scared for her and had enough.

I lay in bed at 2 a.m. and thought, "It's time to let it go," and in the middle of the night, I emailed two people. "Here's an offer you'd be foolish to turn down. It's yours as soon as you're ready."

October 2015, we handed the keys over—and have never looked back!

We finally had time to breathe and focus on health, family, and Monsters.

Until...2016. Becky's dad, who was her mom's primary caretaker, had a stroke. X-rays also uncovered that he had stage four lung cancer that had spread to his bones. This news came just days before Becky's folks were scheduled to move into a nice, new assisted living facility where they looked forward to amenities rivaling the nicest cruise ship.

After only a few months, Becky's dad passed away, and six months later, her mom followed.

Sorrow sunk into our bones, and through it all, we pushed on. We had businesses to run, staff to provide for, and a family to raise.

Over this decade and a half, we encountered challenges that tested us in ways I wouldn't wish on anyone else. We bent, and, at times, we felt broken. Through it all, we found hope and remained faithful in God, in ourselves and in those around us.

We were forced to step back, pivot, and let go. We let go of our pride when we needed to rely on family and friends to help us with meals or getting the kids here and there. We let go of control at work when health concerns prohibited us from being at the office or traveling with the crew. And we let go of our stubbornness when we realized we needed help in our marriage.

Above all, the values of humility and gratitude carried us through it all. And love.

9: Washed Out

"Will this step just be another misstep
To tarnish whatever the legacy, love, or respect, I've garnered?"
Eminem

Not only do we use the lens of the family for decision-making pur-
poses, our community—the one we've created and the one where
we live—is a big part of our lives. Because Becky and I grew up in a small
town and loved it, it felt natural to have our Monsters' headquarters in
Old Ellicott City, a historic town nestled between the Tiber and Patapsco rivers. It's home to St. Paul's Catholic Church, where Babe Ruth
married his wife, and the oldest B&O train station in the country.

Ellicott City, formerly Ellicott's Mills, was settled in 1771 by three
Quaker brothers, originally from Bucks County, Pennsylvania. The old
town hosted Civil War troops and saw the body of slain President Lincoln pass through it on its way from Washington, D.C., to Springfield,
Illinois.

But we didn't start in an office. Monsters' headquarters was first on
my kitchen table! Cue Drake's *Started From the Bottom*. Working at the
heart of our home wasn't exactly easy, and I quickly realized I needed
a consistent place to work.

I made a trip to Home Depot and picked up some two by fours and
nails, six four-by-eight panels of dry erase whiteboard, and I framed
out three walls in the unfinished part of my basement. I had the cable
company add a phone line and internet cable, so I could plug in and I

set up shop. After our first event in Philly, I added a large map of the United States to one wall to plan out our first tour.

For the first year or so, I worked in that makeshift office in my unfinished basement until I could no longer take the absence of daylight. We then turned our garage into an office, which had space for two desks, one for Becky and one for me. We added file cabinets and storage and felt we were living the high life!

Becky & Andy in Monsters' garage office

At this point in our business, everything we owned and used to produce Monsters fit in our garage office. We had three Fender Passport portable sound systems that I bought at Guitar Center, three CD players (I wonder how many people reading this remember CD players), one backdrop, a variety of forms, and office supplies. And let's not forget the limited merchandise that we had spread from the office into our dining room.

I would ship our sound systems and other equipment in their original cardboard boxes via UPS or FedEx to each city and then back to our house after each event. But the merchandise was another story.

In the beginning, a regular crew of family traveled to each city: Angie, her husband Aaron, Gina, her partner LT, Becky and me. To save money on shipping, we stuffed as much merchandise as we could fit in oversized duffle bags, and we each checked two bags on the flights. We carried on all personal items.

Nowadays, our production equipment (which is still modest compared to some other events) encompasses numerous road cases and several pallets that move across the country from city to city in a full-size tractor-trailer.

Even when we hired our first full-time employee, a long-time friend, and former co-worker Gene Burdette, I continued to work at home and he worked out of his house. We'd meet in between or occasionally at the dance studio.

The business grew, but we couldn't justify or afford to take on the expense of another office just for Gene and me. It wasn't until we hired our second full-time employee, Courtney, that we moved operations out of the house, and even then, we just moved into the teacher lounge at our new and expanded dance studio for B.Funk.

This new arrangement worked just fine until about 4:30 each day when people started to arrive for classes, and the teachers needed their space.

Then in the summer of 2013, our staff grew yet again with the addition of Caroline McCabe, who had interned with us during the summer of her senior year at Florida State. It quickly became evident that the teacher lounge wasn't going to work much longer, but we survived one more year in the studio lounge until the fall of 2014 when we made a move.

Historic Main Street Ellicott City was a natural choice for our new office. It was two minutes from home so we could walk or bike to work. There were restaurants and great coffee shops. We loved living in that awesome community.

We checked out a few options before happening upon the perfect spot with windows overlooking the river. The office was only about 600 square feet but had an open floor plan, space for a small kitchenette, and one bathroom. We loved it! We settled in, and Main Street became our new home. To give you a visual about how gorgeous Old Ellicott City's Main Street was, it made it to the final four cities vying for the 2015 title of Best Main Streets in America.

Historic Ellicott City lies between the valleys of the Tiber and Patapsco rivers. The historic district includes the Ellicott City Station, which is the oldest surviving train station in the United States, having been built in 1830 as the first terminus of the original B&O Railroad line. Main Street pitches down toward the Patapsco River.

Floods historically plagued the area, especially when hurricanes hit and caused the Patapsco to surge over its banks. The railroad bridge kept tally of the high watermarks, the highest associated with Hurricane Agnes in 1972.

On June 30, 2016, I was in Los Angeles for our annual Monsters Show and Finale. My phone battery had died. When I got to my hotel room around two in the morning (Pacific time) and plugged my phone in, a barrage of missed calls and text messages lit up the phone's screen.

"Are you guys okay?"

"Is your house okay?"

"Are Becky and the boys safe?"

I had no clue what was happening back home until I opened one text that had a video of the flash flooding. It showed water coursing down Main Street, taking with it cars and the lives of two people. They called it the "thousand-year flood," saying the flash flooding was an anomaly, brought on by the torrential rains that had dumped more than six inches of water in two hours. Unlike previous floods, which were the result of the Patapsco rising, this flood came from above the town and a minor tributary coursing through it.

Many homes and businesses were completely destroyed. The asphalt completely buckled, and water eroded the foundations of many buildings. We felt fortunate that our family and staff were safe and believed that our offices had sustained minor damage.

Four days after the flood, I returned home from Los Angeles. We knew from the news and videos online that the damage to our town had been devastating, but nothing could have prepared us for what we saw.

Access to Main Street was extremely limited for safety reasons—only business and property owners with proper credentials were permitted to set foot on what had been Main Street. Authorized staff drove us on four-wheelers from the county offices to our office location. Allotted only ten minutes to grab essentials, we took with us a couple of trash bags, masks, and gloves.

As we neared the top of Main Street, the air changed. It smelled of mold and stagnant water. The day was hot and humid. The front door of our office was ajar, with four inches of mud and sand washed up on either side of it.

I scraped enough debris away to push the door open. Immediately the stench of mold and sewage hit our noses. We quickly put on our masks before taking a few steps inside.

My stomach sank, and I thought, "Thank God we were in L.A."

Everything, except a few framed items on the walls, was pushed into jumble at the far left end of the office. Mud and small branches littered the floor. A section of the wall was pushed through to the adjoining office. All of the riverside windows had shattered, allowing over four feet of water to rush inside.

Desks were overturned. The refrigerator was upside down. When I opened the frig door, I nearly threw up—it was filled with thick brown water and rotting leftovers. I stepped outside to settle my stomach.

A visual inspection revealed most of our stuff, except for the television. It was nowhere to be found. Had it been looted? Had it floated away through the open window?

We realized that there wasn't much we could do and didn't linger, grabbing a few pictures before making our way back to the four-wheeler.

As the days and weeks went by, we realized how truly lucky we were in so many ways. All the stuff we lost could be replaced. How fortunate for us that we could work from anywhere, and our business would move on. WE WOULD REBUILD.

EC Strong

Monsters HQ destroyed in Main St. Flood

Oddly enough, we found a temporary home in the Warehouse at Camden Yards, where I had worked back in college for the Orioles. A friend whose daughter took dance classes at B.Funk heard of our situation and offered us space in their financial firm.

We stayed there for almost six months until our landlord had refinished our office, and we could move back in. This time, we replaced the hand-me-down desks and office equipment that we had accumulated from home with all new items.

Becky and I moved back to the refurbished office while our staff continued working at the temporary space. We wanted to surprise them with a big reopening reveal, which we did, and they loved it.

At this point, we, along with most of our community, were committed to rebuilding. The 2016 flood was called the "thousand-year flood," and so many people poured their hearts and souls into making Main Street bigger and better than ever, a regional destination that would earn us that title of best Main Street in America.

It was incredibly inspiring to see people come together the way our town did. Our County Executive Alan Kittleman, a Republican, and our Democratic Councilperson, Jon Weinstein, worked brilliantly together, putting aside politics and spending countless hours on the ground to support their constituents and neighbors. They gave us hope and modeled how our elected officials should–and could–work together. For a while, we got back to business as usual.

Then came Memorial Day weekend, 2018–May 27. Another storm dumped eight inches of rain within two hours. Flash flooding was occurring all over the Baltimore area.

I was driving on I-95 South, heading home from Aberdeen, Maryland, where Beckett, our youngest, had just played his heart out in a baseball tournament at The Ripken Experience. My phone started to blow up with calls and texts.

Rachel, one of our staff members, called and said, "Main Street is flooding again."

I couldn't (and almost didn't) believe her. Even if it was true, I thought, it won't be as bad as last time. A thousand years hadn't passed! It had only been two years, and the unimaginable was happening, and, this time, it was worse.

We were about ten minutes from home when we got stopped by a Baltimore County police officer. Catonsville had flooded as well, and the access road to our home was closed.

My thoughts went immediately to my parents. My dad was dealing with congestive heart failure, and they could not afford to be stranded at their house if there was an urgent need for medical attention. No matter what I tried, I couldn't get to them. Fortunately, I spoke to them, and the rest of my family; they were all okay.

"Beckett, we'll stay in a hotel tonight if we can't get through," I said. We stopped at the local grocery store and grabbed some toiletries.

A few hours later, we tried another road. Success! We got to my parents' house and then home.

Reports that one person was missing were confirmed. We later learned that he'd lost his life in the flood. The videos were horrific, and I knew that we were in for a shock.

The officials were experienced after the 2016 flooding, so we were able to access the space a little easier the second time around. Again, we signed in, got our credentials, and made our way to Main Street on a four-wheeler, this time departing from a local church.

Drew joined Becky and me on this trip. Unlike the surge of pride and commitment to rebuilding after the earlier flood, we felt sad and defeated. This flood was not a fluke, thousand-year flood that we could forget about again and move on. We suddenly faced a new reality that our town, our family's go-to spot to walk for dinner or ice cream, would never be the same.

The second I walked into our office, I knew we would not be returning. I could not in good conscience knowingly put my kids or our staff in harm's way. No assurances felt valid about saving our beloved Main Street from being devastated again.

Our space was caked with a thick layer of mud. Every window was shattered. Numerous laptops, hard drives, and competition judging equipment were all gone.

What made this experience even worse was that, just a few weeks earlier, I'd discovered a box of Monsters of HipHop archives in my basement. I had also brought to the office a few other special items, including an "Ellicott City Strong" railroad tie that I had been given after the 2016 flood, a rotary dial phone belonging to my grandparents, and the microphone from their roller skating rink.

I found the box upside down, halfway buried in mud and sand. It was completely soaked, and mold had begun to grow. In fact, mold had started to grow nearly everywhere.

We salvaged signed concert programs that had been on the walls, and a bottle of rum that I had given to Gene. I finally located the telephone and microphone, which was the only bright spot on that horrible day. Once again, I felt grateful that none of us were there when the flash flood happened.

The 2018 flood brought with it a new reality and very different emotions. After '16, I feverishly bought into rebuilding Main Street and being part of its historic turnaround. The second time, we felt defeated and, honestly, lucky to be alive. Had we been in the office during either flood, I'm not sure we would have gotten out.

Our office had been on the riverside behind E.C. Pops. There was no second floor and no other places to scramble when the floodwaters hit. Just the thoughts of what might have happened convinced us it was time to abandon historic Old Ellicott City and find a new office space to call home.

We spent a couple of months working in a temporary space that had been graciously donated by the Abrams Development Group in Columbia, Maryland, while we searched for space to open our new headquarters.

A quick real estate search led me to a building for sale in Catonsville, only a few minutes from home and just down the road from our old Main Street office. Dubbed "Music City Maryland," Catonsville felt like a natural fit for our hip hop headquarters. If you're ever in town, stop by and take a selfie with our homage mural to Christopher George Latore Wallace, also known as The Notorious B.I.G., Biggie Smalls, or Biggie.

Becky has said that the creation of Monsters of HipHop was something of a dream, so it seemed fitting that we would share Biggie's "It Was All a Dream" lyric on the side of our new office.

Monsters new headquarters, 2019

10: Giving Back

"Opportunity dances with those already on the dance floor."
H. Jackson Brown, Jr.

My older brother Alan died in 1990 after a valiant, five-year battle with leukemia. At the time, he was a sophomore at Penn State University, and he was my hero.

Despite the challenges he faced, Alan always kept a positive attitude. His wisdom and courage, even though he was only fifteen when diagnosed with leukemia, still astounds me.

When we learned that I was nearly a perfect match, I was immediately ready to do whatever I needed to do. At 12 years of age, I donated some of my bone marrow to him and how I wished it could have saved him. It's because of his example and death that I'm driven to make a positive difference in the lives of the people we interact with, young and old.

Alan and my family taught me to put others first, so it has always been important to us to give back whenever we can.

From the moment we started in business with the dance studio, we sought out community service opportunities. The American Heart Association, Leukemia & Lymphoma Society, ARC, The White House Easter Egg Roll, pro sports events, and many more—we took advantage of any opportunity to get our students involved.

When we opened B.Funk in 1999, Becky partnered with ARC of Howard County to provide free dance classes for dancers with special needs.

She was inspired to start the program by her cousin, Stephanie, who had Down's Syndrome and loved to dance. The kids had an absolute blast, and so did Becky, so it was disappointing when ARC was unable to continue to participate in the program due to transportation issues.

Kassidy Bright with eMpower Dancer

There was a void left after the special needs program fizzled out. Then, long time Monsters' dancer and Show alumni, Kassidy Bright, rekindled the idea of a special needs program and offered to teach a class on our convention tour. In keeping with Monsters' mission, these unique "eMpower" classes allow dancers with special needs the chance to express themselves in a fun and safe environment.

Thanks to Kassidy, who has a unique gift for teaching this program, the first eMpower event was held in Atlanta, and we had literally thirty or forty kids arrive on a party bus from Alabama. The free class lasted two hours, during which time they learned choreography, had a freestyle session, and enjoyed some pizza!

Now, we organize our eMpower program in several cities in conjunction with Monsters' conventions with the support of many generous supporters.

Many years ago, at a very young age, our middle son Cooper expressed a desire to end homelessness. We were so impressed that ever since that day, we have made a point to participate in making and distributing lunches for the homeless in our community. Thanks to an amazing volunteer, Ms. Eileen, we were introduced to the Westside Men's Shelter, where we deliver 120 lunches a few times per year.

Military service members have also been a target of our support as we have personally had numerous veterans in our own families. In many tour cities, we set up collections of unused hotel toiletries that are then donated to local homeless veterans.

Of course, when life happens, and special opportunities arise, we feel a responsibility to respond. That's what happened in the fall of 2019 when we received a call from a mom requesting a refund. When we asked why, she explained that her ten-year-old son Nick had been diagnosed with a rare form of cancer and would not be able to attend our D.C. event. When I heard his story, my stomach sank and I called Becky right away.

We all know how much cancer sucks, but to hit a vibrant ten-year-old just doesn't seem right. We reached out to his dance studio owner, Kim, to find out how we could help and ultimately decided to set up a workshop to help raise funds for the family. I recalled the outpouring of support for my family and knew it was the right thing to do.

Monsters Battle for Nick was a huge success thanks to the generosity of choreographers Laura Edwards and Candace Brown, who donated their time to teach. Nearly 100 dancers showed up plus folks who had only heard about Nick's story. The main man, Nick himself, was in attendance and danced his heart out as long as he could. The support and energy were overwhelming, and thanks to the incredible dance community, we raised $7,000 in that quick pop-up event.

Nick's got a long fight ahead, but I have no doubt that he will be back dancing as strong as ever!

It's amazing to see the power of a strong community that works together toward a common goal. Such a simple concept, right?

Becky, Candace Brown, Nick Shalin, Laura Edwards & Andy at Monsters Battle for Nick

11: Bloopers

"Believe when I say I'm no better than you,
except when I rap, so I guess that ain't true."
The Beastie Boys

Two-thousand and eight nearly brought us to our knees. The economy tanked. Housing prices fell. Layoffs were rampant. And still, B.Funk Dance Company thrived. By then, we had about 500 students.

Monsters of HipHop had established its reputation among top choreographers and the people wanting to hire them. You might say Monsters brought credibility to hip hop on the convention circuit. That year, our convention tour took us to seventeen cities with, on average, between 700 and 1,000 dancers attending each city's convention. Our reputation in the hip hop community kept climbing.

Fox's show, *So You Think You Can Dance*, had runaway success featuring both hip hop and contemporary dance styles. We started to think that we might replicate the success we'd experienced with hip hop and parlay into something similar for contemporary dance. In 2009, we booked nine cities for a new event we called Monsters of Contemporary, selecting specific cities known for their love of contemporary dance.

On a good weekend, sixty to eighty people showed up for the contemporary conventions. Those who attended benefited greatly because of the low attendance, they received nearly one-to-one corrections from the top contemporary talent. Monsters of Contemporary faculty included renowned choreographers such as Tovaris Wilson, Sonya Tayeh, Wes Veldink, Peter Chu, William Wingfield, Jillian Meyers, and more. I couldn't fathom why more people wouldn't want to be a part of this.

We bled money, city after city. It made no sense. We struggled with it because the feedback and environment were phenomenal. Finally, after about two years of planning and praying that contemporary dancers would see the light and flock to our convention, I called a big studio in Minneapolis, Minnesota, that was known for contemporary and several others throughout the country and asked the owners for feedback.

"Why aren't more dancers coming?" I asked. "Those who have raved about the experience. What am I missing?"

Turns out: I was missing a key element. The contemporary dance community wanted the competition—the exact opposite of how the hip hop convention was successfully structured.

Monsters' was all about career development and training. It has never been about winning trophies. So we let contemporary go—realizing that this style wasn't the core focus of our business.

We had become increasingly exhausted, physically, and mentally. Most importantly, we realized how much we had slipped on the attention we previously paid to the hip hop events.

We learned a big lesson—not to mention an expensive one. Confucious said, "A man who chases two rabbits catches none."

Ultimately, we cut nine cities from the next year's tour, focused solely on our hip hop niche, and made more money with fewer cities. I'd like to tell you that we made only great decisions from there forward, but that wouldn't be the truth. Let's just say I've learned more from poor decisions than I have from good ones!

For example, Monsters Dance Music. Never heard of it? I'm not surprised! Like other entrepreneurs, I get a lot of ideas. One of them was to leverage the amazing skills of our talented faculty, many of whom are songwriters, singers, and musicians. My idea was to write and produce great music and upload the videos to YouTube as a way to promote Monsters and showcase our incredible talent. I wanted to make Monsters a one-stop-shop for the professional artistic community—which, in many ways, it still is!

I reached out to two choreographers on our faculty and told them about my idea. At first, they thought I was kidding. After several months, after me pushing for a budget, they realized I was serious.

I sat with Chonique Sneed at the Double T Diner by the studio late one night, and I asked her, "How's your music coming along?" What followed was an amazing collaboration with Cho, Luther Brown, and music insider K.O. The Legend.

LET IT GO Album Cover

The first single we produced was called "Let It Go"(not the Disney version). This incredible first song went platinum on Spotify and took the dance industry by storm. Quickly, video after video appeared on YouTube of people teaching to the song, competing to it, and being performed in hundreds of freestyle videos.

Our "Let It Go" was used in two films: one in New Zealand and one in New York. It was also featured on *So You Think You Can Dance*. Seriously, our first song had something like seven license agreements!

The next two songs we did with Chonique formed a sort of trilogy with the first song. The process was great fun. After doing much of the same thing for many years, this new challenge, the opportunity to learn a new industry, and work with these incredibly talented people gave me a renewed enthusiasm for my work.

It was also incredibly time-consuming. I realized that it would take a painfully long time to recoup our investment...with money coming in like a trickle but going out like a flood.

Monsters Dance Music was a fun project, and one I'm incredibly grateful we tried. We realized that all the time and money we had invested in it ultimately pulled us away from our core business once again.

Besides the Contemporary conventions and Music projects, we've had plenty of other exciting diversions along the way. Here are a few highlights:

- ✧ Becky and Andy produce tour auditions for Janet Jackson, 2007

- ✧ Disney Grad Night with the Jabbawockeez, 2008 (their first commercial booking after winning the inaugural season of *America's Best Dance Crew*)

- ✧ Monsters expanded to New Zealand where Becky and Andy Funk renewed their wedding vows, 2009

- ✧ Monsters Cancun, 2010

- ✧ Monsters on the Move Foundation is created in 2010-2014 as a 501-c3, providing over $100,000 in four years to underprivileged dancers.

- ✧ Monsters partners with ABC's Extreme Makeover Home Edition, 2011

- ✧ Sea Monsters Caribbean Cruises, 2011 and 2012 (hosted Monsters on a Royal Caribbean Cruise)

- ✧ The Choreographer's Cup, 2014 (Awarded Robert Green, a top prize of $5,000 for unique choreography competition)

- ✧ Collaboration on tour with Sony to discover vocal talent, 2015
- ✧ Casting opportunities for companies including Comcast, Disney, HP, Universal, The Maury Povich Show, and Sony Screen Gems

All of these opportunities have made for an incredible ride and taught us so much along the way, but one, in particular, provided a pivotal shift in our decision-making moving forward.

Over the years, we had received numerous scholarship requests for Monsters and honored many of them based on need. After a few years, though, we thought our impact would be much greater through a non-profit designation. We set up *Monsters on the Move Foundation* (MOVE), a 501-c3 organization that provided scholarships for underprivileged dancers. As part of their application, they had to propose how they would pay it forward as we wanted to spread the feeling of giving back.

In four years, we awarded over a hundred thousand dollars, with less than ten percent raised from outside donors. Plus, we continued to provide scholarships to Monsters out of pocket as the IRS did not allow us to use MOVE funds for people to attend our own events.

The concept and impact were great; however, we completely underestimated the time and work required to effectively operate a nonprofit business, so we reluctantly closed down Monsters on the Move. This was an extremely difficult but necessary decision.

We jumped into the non-profit arena too quickly and somewhat arrogantly, and once again found out the hard way that we needed to re-evaluate our thought process on new projects. We learned that once we focused solely on our core business and allowed ourselves the appropriate time to make things happen, that's when Monsters' growth catapulted. We were no longer splitting efforts and depleting resources.

From 2009 to 2015, there were numerous times that we tried new things and then let them go. You could call some of them failures, I guess, and that's fine, but I also realized more than failures, they were instead opportunities to grow and sharpen our mission.

Onward and upward, I like to say! Lemonade anyone?

12: No Turning Back

"Never become so involved with something that it blinds you.
Never forget where you from, someone will remind you."
DMX

When I look back now, I don't know how we ran two successful businesses while raising three boys, each of whom had their own activities and interests. We have the luxury of looking back and seeing how far we've come and prioritizing where we're going.

My family comes first, always. I still work early in the morning and late into the night, so I can take my boys to school in the morning and pick them up in the afternoon every day. I volunteer at school more and in their activities. I act as the disc jockey at baseball games or school dances—I guess everyone thinks since we operate a hip hop dance convention that I can handle it, and I don't like to disappoint!

In the past, I would only miss conventions if I absolutely couldn't go due to a funeral or health issue at home. Now, I choose to stay home more often so I can be present at as many of my family's events and activities as possible.

For several years, our oldest son, Drew, desperately wanted to play travel baseball. We just couldn't fathom how we would fit it into our schedules, so we told him no.

After 2011, things shifted. At twelve years old, Drew received the invitation—and a "yes" from us to play travel baseball. Sharing the experience of him playing baseball in Cooperstown at Dreams Park was simply fantastic. We also didn't wait and allowed Beckett to do travel ball as well. For a few spring and summers, when they were both playing, we spent six to seven days per week on ball fields, and it was awesome!

In the summer of 2019, Cooper, our middle child, played the lead role in a local theatre production of Aladdin, and a day later, we revisited Cooperstown, where we saw Beckett hit his first home run! (All those years of practicing logistics have really come in handy for managing conflicting kids' activities!) All of this took place while Monsters Show rehearsals were underway in LA. Again, it was all possible because of our terrific Monsters staff who covered for us.

I've also learned to temper my enthusiasm every time we have a new bright idea. In 2009, we nearly signed a ten-year lease on a 25,000 square foot building in Burbank, California. The space was amazing. It included a green screen studio and massive white syc perfect for filming, a separate building that we planned to turn into a studio apartment, and a parking lot.

We had visited multiple times, negotiated the lease with some great incentives, and had a final lease in hand about to sign. We had researched and spoken to potential staff who would run the place, going so far as to create a rough schedule of operations.

As I thought about operating a business from 3,000 miles away, pressure and anxiety grew. There would be more coast-to-coast trips, among other challenges. I had reached a place where I felt like we were on top of the world and could accomplish anything we set out to do. While I believe having that space would have resulted in a successful venture for us, I decided that we were right where we needed to be at the time and decided to call off the deal. The instant I declined the lease, I felt a tremendous weight lifted from my chest. Saying "no" to myself never felt so good! And that was just the start of a shift.

By taking better care of ourselves and prioritizing our family and using them as the lens through which we make decisions, we've been able to grow and sustain our business more than when I was hustling so hard. I highly recommend adopting something similar for yourself!

Don't get me wrong, this business is always a hustle, we're just a lot smarter about it now.

In the beginning, we lived by that Rihanna lyric *"work work work work work"* and now, thanks to the hardest working staff in the business, I feel like we've been able to let go and trust them to take care of things. We still work on the business daily in some way but have made it a point to find time for ourselves as well. Whether it's going for lunch together, scheduling a massage, or taking in a matinee on a Monday afternoon, we're living lives outside of the business, too.

In 2014, I applied for a program called Leadership Howard County (LHC), whose mission it is to connect leaders from business, non-profit, and government to create awareness and understanding to stimulate action for the benefit of the community, the workplace, and for the individual's personal and professional growth.

Our banker had been encouraging me for a couple of years to join, and I kept putting it off with the same excuse, "I don't have the time." I worked, traveled for Monsters, helped with the kids' activities, and did my best to keep up with Monsters on the Move, the non-profit that we started just a few years earlier.

I knew that a program like LHC would be the kick in the pants that I needed both professionally and professionally. I also knew that my schedule was not going to lighten up, so I gave in and applied.

I was fortunate to be invited to join the Leadership Premier Class of 2014, and I can honestly say it has been one of the most fulfilling and inspiring business decisions I've ever made.

During the nine months in the program, I had the opportunity to meet and work with executives and leaders from all walks of life as well as a variety of industries, including education, government, health care, community service, and non-profits.

The most transformative lesson for me occurred as part of the United Way *Walk a Mile* exercise. If you ever have an opportunity to experience this, I highly recommend it. I thought I had empathy, but it wasn't until I simulated a day in the life of one Baltimore family that I realized how truly fortunate I am.

After we'd completed *Walk a Mile*, there was a group reflection where we shared how we felt and what we learned. A key takeaway for me was that, although we talk a great deal about making a positive impact on our communities, we often don't follow-through and make it happen. What can we do to improve even one person's life?

I recall sitting there with a pit in my stomach. A guilty feeling set in thinking about my privilege and the reality of the Baltimore family whose lives we just had a glimpse of. I raised my hand and said, "We talk about how much this has affected us, but what are we going to do about it?" At that moment, numerous classmates echoed the same sentiment, and from that point forward, every time we met as a group, we did some sort of collection or donation for a group in need.

I thought back to Jamie McDonald's presentation, where she described a helicopter hovering over a flood disaster. From high in the air, it looked like total devastation. From afar, it looked too overwhelming—there was no real way to help. But, as the helicopter descended, a patch of dry land appeared and closer still, you could see movement.

Then when the helicopter reached the ground, there was a family walking on the street. They carried a backpack full of salvaged items, they held a baby in their arms, and their dog trotted behind them. You realize that you can help one family, and, by doing so, you've changed their lives for the better. If you'd have stayed high in the air, you might have flown right past.

This parable may sound simple, but it really is that easy. I used to feel tremendous pressure to have a global impact. I never thought that what we were doing was enough. Nowadays, I take pride in the impact we're having at Monsters, and in the communities we visit.

Most importantly, you've got to take that first step. Don't stop with the idea. Speak up. Question. Take action.

13: WE ARE MONSTERS

"Life without dreaming is a life without meaning."
Wale

People often ask me, "Where did the name *Monsters* come from?" When we came up with the idea of assembling ten of the world's top choreographers from the world of hip hop, we knew it would be a monumental task. The term Monsters signified those who are larger than life at the top of their game.

A few years after we started, there was a shiny new and eerily similar convention on the scene that presented new competition for us. We hired a high priced marketing agency from Los Angeles to take a look at our company and make recommendations on how we could improve and get to the next level in our business.

After interviewing our staff and researching our target audience, they came back with their report. Their biggest finding?? They wanted us to change our name. *"Monsters of HipHop* is too scary for parents to want to send their children," they said. Are you kidding me? I paid how many thousand dollars for that? The biggest lesson learned from that experiment was to trust in ourselves and our ideas. Needless to say, we stuck with the name.

From day one, we have sought out the most influential and respected working choreographers and creative directors in the world. *Respected* is the key word here. All the credits or followers in the world do not make an incredible person who can inspire someone else for good.

It's funny how it started out as a family business with the support of friends and so many in the community who helped me through some of the darkest times early in life. No wonder Monsters has naturally grown into its own big FAMILY! But who makes up our family?

Monsters Faculty lookout for the dancers like parents care for their own children. Much more than employing them, they mentor and take them under their wing to set them up for success. For many young dancers moving away from home for their first time in Los Angeles, Monsters choreographers have become like second parents to them. "Mama Rhap," "LuDaddy"? Those nicknames are no coincidence! And there are so many others like Kevin Maher who has sponsored numerous international dancers, Chonique and Lisette who molded and mentored countless dancers over the years through their Creating Opportunities program.

One of my favorite casting opportunities came thanks to the incomparable Jamal Sims. He has put his stamp on countless films such as *Aladdin*, the *Step Up* films, *Descendants,* and dozens more. But the best was when he called on us to help with casting for *Hannah Montana: The Movie* back in 2009. Walt Disney Studios was holding their auditions in L.A. but filming in Nashville, so Jamal reached out to see if we could put the word out to dancers on the East Coast.

This wasn't the first time that Jamal called me about dancers, actually. That came before the first *Step Up* film that was shot in Baltimore in 2006. He called and asked if I had "Blondie's" number. Of course, he was talking about Laura Edwards, who he remembered from on tour and also from the inaugural Monsters Show cast.

Anyway, back to Hannah Montana...

We pitched the idea to Disney to use our Monsters Greenville stop as an East Coast audition, and we became the official East Coast Casting for the film. From that audition alone, Jamal booked sixteen dancers who appeared in the film, many of whom it was their first professional job.

The best part came a few weeks later when Jamal called again and said he needed eight to ten dancers in Nashville the next week. I said jokingly, "Would you take my wife?"

Without laughing, he said, "Absolutely, Becky would be great for this."

Do you know she still gets checks from that movie? (Fun fact: her dance partner in the film was none other than JaQuel Knight.)

We lost track of how many dancers our faculty have hired long ago because it happens all of the time. We see our mission in action in nearly every television or award show, artist tour, or film that includes dancers. Jamal is just one of our amazing faculty who look out for Monsters dancers regularly. From day one, they bought into our mission 100%, and that's what makes our faculty so special. Through Monsters, we have built a clear pathway to the industry.

If the faculty are the parents, our Monsters Show Alumni must be the kids! That's how we see them, at least. From the moment they step into their first show rehearsal, they form a bond that can never be broken. They are brothers and sisters for life.

Life in L.A. is not easy, particularly as self-employed, and often starving artists. One thing is for sure. Monsters kids are never alone. This is never more evident than each summer when they come together to reconnect at the Monsters Show in the alumni performance or just to show their support for one another and also for the newest cast members.

Our alumni take great pride and responsibility in their role as part of the Monsters legacy, constantly giving back. So many of them have taken the lead to follow in the footsteps of their mentors by passing their own knowledge down to the next generation—alumni like Andye J who created "Queen Domination" to empower women in dance and Lee Daniel who created "Men of Distinction," an all-male performance-intensive and movement forum.

Part of what makes the Monsters Show unique is the physically and mentally grueling process that they go through. It's this process of personal discovery that prepares our alumni for anything the industry might throw at them, and through it all, they lift one another up. And this never ends.

We recently had the honor of witnessing Laura Edwards' wedding held in Maryland, where over thirty Monsters Show alumni flew in from all over the world to attend. Becky and I watched in awe of those kids and their love for one another.

So if the faculty are the parents and the alumni are the kids, who else makes up this crazy amazing family?

A good family is much stronger with a community to support them. Without the dancers, studio owners, and parents who have entrusted us with enhancing their dance education throughout the years, we wouldn't have a business. So I offer a HUGE thank you to every individual who has ever come through our doors!

Last, but not least, none of the above would be possible without a staff of hard-working, extremely talented people to carry out the day-to-day operation of our mission. We could surely hire warm bodies to answer phones and process registrations but our customers are more than a number. We once received a survey response to the question, "What's your favorite part of Monsters?" with the answer "the friendliness of Gene." Our staff, like Gene, are the fuel that keeps the engine running and the reason our customers feel more like family than a number.

Monsters staff have a reputation like this for always going above and beyond to ensure that everyone leaves feeling better than when they arrived. Lord knows we've had our fair share of crises that have taken us away from the business. In those times, I have never questioned that it was taken care of. That's family!

I can't help but think of some of our long-time staff and how they came to work with us. David Efaw, Cheri Chandler, and Kathy Cheek all used to bring their kids to Monsters and they sat in the ballrooms watching them grow up year-after-year with us. Over time, they saw an area whether it was with sound equipment and DJing or merchandise and they jumped right in to help, ultimately joining us on staff. Each time they expressed how much they enjoyed being around our family and the feeling was always mutual.

I'd be remiss if I didn't properly acknowledge another special family lead by @BgPopa, Brett Goebel. Brett brought his daughter Parris and her crew (Request Crew) all the way from New Zealand to Monsters Phoenix over twelve years ago. I recall a chatter among faculty and staff about this curly-haired girl wearing yellow basketball shorts who was killing every routine. She was different—her motivation, passion and genuine love for what she was doing shined brighter than her shorts.

I'm not sure if they were stalking us or if it was a coincidence but after the convention, we both ended up at the same restaurant. If you recall from my childhood, food has always been super important so I think that's truly where our relationship blossomed! Turns out we would share numerous meals together over the next decade—a traditional feast at their home in NZ, my Mom's famous roast beef dinner at our house in Maryland, and Ms. Peaches Soul Food in North Hollywood, CA.

Back in Phoenix, I had expressed how visiting New Zealand was on my bucket list, and immediately without hesitation, Brett wrapped his big frame around my shoulder, squeezing hard and said confidently, "You'll be there soon!" The following year, I checked off that bucket list item when Brett, Parris, and their family hosted us in Auckland for our first international convention.

Brett has been a friend and ambassador for Monsters in more ways than one, often acting as a mentor in business and marketing but always reminding me of how important family is!

There is an African Proverb that I think sums up best how I feel about Monsters and all of those who have joined us on our journey, "If you want to go fast, go alone. If you want to go far, go together."

Of course, we're proud of the mark we've made in this industry (so far), but Monsters is so much more than a powerful dance convention.

We've trained tens of thousands of dancers over the years from all over the world, but the blessings our family has received as a result of Monsters are incalculable.

Angie, Gina, LT, and Aaron—you all played key roles in making Monsters' magical—without you, none of this would have been possible.

My biggest inspirations are my parents, Gene and Joyce, who have given me the best life possible. They have withstood unbearable challenges of losing a child and difficult financial circumstances as a result of years of health issues.

Despite all this, I never felt like our family life suffered. We didn't always have annual family vacations, but we made plenty of memories. Whether it was driving remote-controlled cars on the ice-covered Laurel Lake, or swimming in the pool that my brother received from the Make-A-Wish Foundation (essentially for me), we made the best of every situation.

I never knew the financial hardship my parents endured, only the outpouring of support from the community, and their never-ending love. My parents did an amazing job of "protecting us" from the challenges they faced and always moved onward and upward!

Becky's Grandma Mary used to make a special Italian pepperoni sauce that we all tried to duplicate, but we could never get it right. Monsters is a lot like that. Many ingredients go into making Monsters great, but you can't replace our family!

14: Monsters Legacy

"Climb the ladder of success, escalator-style."
Notorious B.I.G.

I've thought about the future of Monsters a lot and for a long time. I look at other highly respected convention owners like Joe Tremaine (Tremaine Dance) and Joe Lanteri (New York City Dance Alliance) who have had a tremendous impact on the dance industry. I am grateful for leaders like them who have made their mark and done it respectfully, uniquely, and stood the test of time because of it. When we created Monsters of HipHop, no one else had ever done specifically what we sought out to do. We knew it was a huge risk, but we were determined to do something different and make an impact in our own lane.

Over the years, I'm not gonna lie, there have been times when the next shiny new convention or competition would pop up that would present challenges in terms of faculty, scheduling head to head in the same cities, even spreading rumors that we were canceling cities or selling the business. Each time, Monsters remained strong.

There was one pivotal night several years ago when Becky and I spent about two hours talking with a couple of our faculty members about some of these issues, and I realized that, in those two hours, we could have been focused on making our own brand even better. I slept pretty well that night and woke up even more driven to continue to build on the Monsters legacy. We have no interest in competing with or taking away from anyone else. There are dancers everywhere who live for what we all do, and I firmly believe that working together, being mindful of our uniqueness, we can all succeed in delivering our missions.

For many years, we were a reactionary operation, keeping up with what was right in front of us. More recently, I have been making greater efforts to plan further ahead. I even bought a five-year calendar book with a cover that reads "Get Shit Done" as a constant reminder to stay on my toes. I have events booked three years out or more and a plan, for example, of how we will follow up our first European stop in Dublin in 2020.

Having lived and learned through so much loss over the years in our family, I realize just how precious time truly is, and there is much more to me than being a dance convention producer all of my life. This platform has provided opportunities I never dreamed of as a boy growing up in a small historic town. I've renewed my wedding vows in New Zealand thanks to Brett Goebel and his family and made lifelong friendships with strangers from all over the world.

I am hopeful that I get to enjoy these times with my boys in the future as well. Drew, who is nineteen at the time of this writing, has already expressed a strong desire to become more involved in the family business and potentially take over Monsters one day. In his senior year of high school, he did an internship with us where he traveled to eight cities, shadowed each staff member and worked in nearly every area of the business, fitting in perfectly with everyone he encountered.

Cooper, who is right now fifteen, has already made his mark by inspiring our 15th Anniversary logo redesign with the hidden "M." Haven't noticed it? Check out his rough sketches on the back of a Bob Evans restaurant placemat. His creativity and interest in film and photography could definitely be an asset in the future.

While the jury is still out on Beckett (12), I think he could be the professional dancer of the crew, but for now, it's baseball, ping pong, and fighting the boxing dummy. Of course, he's the one pushing us to stay up to speed on the latest social media platforms, including critiquing every one of our TikTok posts.

Cooper's inspirational sketch for our 15th Anniversary logo redesign

Bob Evans Placemat with Cooper's logo sketch

While I dread the time when the boys are all grown and out of the house, their interest in working with us has given me new life and even greater enthusiasm for the business. I look forward to the time when they bring their life experiences to the table, share new ideas, and help us build the next chapters of Monsters. Of course, they may change their minds entirely, and that's okay too, I just want them to be happy and healthy. I can always dream, right?

The Monsters' legacy is more than Andy or Becky Funk and much more than *just business*. It's family!

Post-Script: Confessions of a (Former) Dog-Hater

"Let me go my way but walk with me
See what I see, watch me then, talk with me
Share my pain, make it a little easier to deal with it."
DMX

Those who know me best know that I have a dark secret past when it comes to dogs: I grew up terrified of them.

It all began when I was around five or six years old. We heard loud, aggressive growling and barking in our backyard. My Dad, brother, and I ran out back to see what was going on and discovered that a neighborhood dog had chased a cat up a tree, but not before taking a bite out of its neck.

My dad chased the dog away, and we eventually got the cat out of the tree by offering it a pan of cold milk. My mom convinced my dad to take the cat to a vet to have it treated. The vet wouldn't keep it, and it wouldn't leave our backyard, so we ended up with our first pet, Morris, the cat.

We had Morris for a few years until my brother got sick, and we could no longer keep him. With Alan's weakened immune system, we couldn't keep a stray cat around, so we had to find him a new home.

While the cat-attacking dog screwed me up, it was really our neighbor's dog that turned me against dogs. One morning I walked out outside intending to ride my bike. My neighbor's dog had his front two paws firmly placed on the frame of my bike, growling and barking at me as if he wanted to take a bite out of MY neck.

I turned and scampered back into the house. My parents were frustrated that the neighbor allowed her dog to do his business in our yard. For forty years, I grew up thinking dogs were evil.

Then came Decker.

My sons lobbied for years for us to get a dog, and I swore, "WE WILL NEVER EVER HAVE A DOG IN THIS HOUSE!" It wasn't until after we sold the dance studio and Becky had more time on her hands that Beckett ramped up the dog requests to the point I thought I'd lose my mind if I didn't at least consider it. Of course, I didn't tell them that!

Becky picked up on my subtle attitude shift and started showing me dog after dog on a variety of rescue sites.

"I WILL NEVER EVER HAVE A DOG IN THIS HOUSE" was what I said the whole time I looked at the rescue sites, and researched breeds.

One day while we were at our Ellicott City office, Becky said, "I reached out to a place called Pet Connect about this cute little dog named Toby that they have listed on their website."

Meanwhile, three desks away in our tiny office, I typed an email to Pet Connect, introducing myself and asked them not to respond to my wife. I wrote that I wanted to surprise my family with Toby for Christmas.

Less than an hour later, I received a frantic phone call from Becky and Drew. "What are you up to?"

The lady at Pet Connect returned Becky's call at the same time she opened my email. Recognizing our last name, she shared, "Oh yes, your husband emailed us about Toby as well."

After forty years of standing my ground and depriving my family of the dog they so badly desired, I was prepared to give in and be the hero. I had decided that I'd pick Toby up on Christmas eve, have my parents keep him for the night, and give my family the biggest surprise of their lives.

The lady proceeded to read my email out loud, while Becky and Drew were on speakerphone. As she read, the conversation grew awkward the moment she realized that she had completely ruined the surprise.

I wanted to cancel the whole thing and go back to the original plan of never EVER getting a dog, but I had passed the point of no return. I agreed to meet Becky and Drew at Toby's foster family's house.

There was no turning back, and it was clear that Becky and Drew were in love. I have to admit Toby was cute, but his sharp puppy teeth freaked me out 'cause I was certain that they would grow into big snapping dog teeth.

We were about to have a dog in our house, and there was nothing I could do to stop it.

We renamed Toby to Decker, which was a combination of all three of the boys' names (D for Drew, eck for Beckett, and er for Cooper).

Here's the most ironic part: Decker is My dog, and I am HIS person. It is undeniable how much he loves me. I am clearly his favorite, and he misses me terribly whenever I'm gone, which sends him into a deep depression.

The reality is this damn dog has changed my life! I once hated dogs, and now he's my best friend. He's an eighty-pound Basset Hound/Great Pyrenees/Labrador/Pitbull mixed mutt, and I freakin love him!

I have maintained all along that "Decker's just alright," sheds too much, whines too much, and that he's more for the boys and Becky. To be honest, I can't imagine my life without my Decker dog. He calms me when I'm stressed, he loves me no matter what, and he's a little bit crazy, which fits in perfectly with our family!

Decker Smalls

Acknowledgments

It's hard to believe that this book has finally come to life! Normally when we Funks have an idea, we jump right in but writing this book started over twenty years ago, and I am incredibly grateful for Deborah (Debby) Kevin for her support, encouragement, and editing talent. Thank you, especially for the brownie recipe story! We will continue to share the goodness every chance we get.

To my family, Becky, Drew, Cooper, and Beckett. I am the luckiest person alive to live in this crazy zoo with all of you. You make me better, stronger, and definitely happier every day of my life! I look forward to a lifetime of adventures with you.

Mom and Dad, you are both an incredible light for so many. You are "Mom and Dad, Nana and Pop" to a lot of people who genuinely love you like their own. You have taught me so much, given me so much, and I couldn't do it without you. Alan was so special because of your love, and I thank you for everything you do for me and everyone else.

Gina, Lori, Angie, and Aaron, we couldn't have gotten off the ground without you. You held us together, and, man, did we have fun lugging all of those merch bags around. Even though you wear more Monster's gear now than you ever did AT THE EVENTS, we love you all, and thank you so much!

Bob and Georgia, Thank you for welcoming me into the family, sharing your beautiful daughter, and encouraging me to embrace the entrepreneurial spirit that I always had in me.

To our entire staff, faculty, dancers, and everyone who has played a part in Monsters' success over the years, thank you!

To Decker, you changed my life! I once hated dogs, but your unconditional love has made me a better human. Thanks, buddy!

Special thanks to Gene, Caroline, David, Kathy, Rachel, Aminya, Nate, Carlos, Jake, Julius, James, Daniel, Sierra, Courtney, Brett, Julia, Elise, Brandon, Mike, Ace, JR Mint, Erin, Kate, Suzy, Terri Hicks, Denise, Rosa, Rachel N, Kenda, Matt, Cheri & Mom Chandler, Jim, and the Philly Crew, Kim B, Kim A, Paul, Bill W, Dane, Greg

And our faculty past and present: Rhapsody James, Luther Brown, Laura Edwards, JaQuel Knight, Marty Kudelka, Parris Goebel, Chonique Sneed, Kevin Maher, Nick DeMoura, Jamal Sims, Lisette Bustamante, Sean Bankhead, Luam, Tony Tzar, Tony Testa, Jaja Vankova, Phi, Kevin Brewer, Gary "Gee" Kendall, Kid Rainen, Ben Chung, Phil Tayag, Chris Styles, Antonio Tran, Joe Larot, and the Jabbawockeez, Calvit Hodge, Brian & Scott Nicholson, Andye J, Robert Green, Kassidy & Kaili Bright, Amari Marshall, Candace Brown, Alex Fetbroth, BJ Paulin, Mel Charlot, Gerran Reese, Lee Daniel, Jared Jenkins, Tatiana Parker, Nate Poole, The Royal Family, The BeatFreaks, Quest Crew, Fanny Pak, Napoleon & Tabitha Dumo, Shawnette Heard, Popin' Pete, Mr. Wiggles, Jermaine Brown, Geo Hubela, Brian Friedman, Dave Scott, Misha Gabriel, Flo-Master, Mr. Freeze, Suga Pop, Fatima Robinson, Travis Payne & Stacy Walker, Teresa Espinosa, Chuck Maldonado, Moncell Durden, Raphael Xavier, Terry Wright, Brian Tanaka, Rosero McCoy, Lyle Beniga, Tucker Barkley, Sandy & Maniek, Kerri Milne, Ian Eastwood, Leon Blackwood, Anze Skrube, Denzel Chisolm, Michelle Vaughn, Sarah Steben, Jade Chynoweth, Aurelia Michel, Marlee Hightower, Hannah Gossett, Boy-Boi, Ryan Chandler, Nika Kljun, Montana Efaw, Natasha Gorrie, Derrell Bullock, Matt Cady, Megan Lawson, Dana Wilson, Tovaris Wilson, Peter Chu, Sonya Tayeh, William Wingfield, Jillian Meyers, Wes Veldink, Phillip Chebeeb, David Moore, Fefe Burgos.

About Andrew Funk

 Thirty years, two businesses and three kids later, Andy's uncommon story is one of perseverance, vision, inspiration, and love. Overcoming challenges of health and loss, a financial recession, and balancing business and family life, Andy and his family have successfully navigated through the tough times and maintained humility and tempered enthusiasm during the best of times.

Andy's commitment to family values, community service, and philanthropy has helped create a reputation that goes far beyond just the dance world. Visit **www.monstersdance.com** for more information and follow us on Instagram at **@**MonstersDance.

Song Lyric Credits

1: "All Things Go." Nicki Minaj, The Pinkprint (2014).

2: "In Due Time." Outkast featuring CeeLo Green, *Soul Food* Soundtrack (1997).

3: "Ultralight Beam." Kanye West, The Life of Pablo (2016).

4: "When I See You Smile." Bad English, Bad English (1989).

5: "Fancy." Drake, Thank Me Later (2010).

6: "Juicy." Notorious B.I.G., Ready to Die (1994).

7: "The 6th Sense." Common, Like Water for Chocolate (2000).

8: "Mind Your Business." Brand Nubian and Grand Puba, The Now Rules File (2009).

9: "Walk on Water (featuring Beyoncé)." Eminem, Revival (2017).

10: H. Jackson Brown, Jr., quote.

11: "Ch-Check It Out." Beastie Boys, Ch-Check It Out (2004).

12: "It's On." DMX, The Professional (1999).

13: Wale quote.

14: "You're Nobody Until Somebody Tries to Kill You." Notorious B.I.G., Life After Death (1997).

Post-Script: "Dogs for Life." DMX, Flesh of My Flesh, Blood of My Blood (1998).

Made in the USA
Columbia, SC
06 February 2020